D0994501

About the Author

Paul Denny was born in Hampshire, following the end of World War II. He emigrated to the South Pacific with his wife and children in his late twenties. He holds a Bachelor of Arts degree in History and Social Anthropology. Now retired after a career in information technology and logistics, he enjoys travelling, reading, writing, and walking. He lives in Auckland with his wife Judy.

Dedication

To Judy as ever

Paul G. Denny

SEARCHING FOR ENDA

AUSTIN MACAULEY
PUBLISHERS LTD.

A CIP catalogue record for this title is available from the British Library.

ISBN 9781785548833 (Paperback)
ISBN 9781785548840 (Hardback)
ISBN 9781785548857 (E-Book)

www.austinmacauley.com

First Published (2016)
Austin Macauley Publishers Ltd.
25 Canada Square
Canary Wharf
London
E14 5LQ

Acknowledgments

"I AM NOT WHAT HAS HAPPENED TO ME.
I AM WHAT I CHOOSE TO BECOME."

Carl. G. Jung

Prologue

Adopted at three months old by a loving and caring couple, I started my early childhood growing up in a small village in middle England. It was springtime 1946 and World War II had ended the previous year. Of course, during the first few years of my life, I had no idea my adopted parents were not my biological mother and father.

When I was four years old, Mum and Dad told me I was going to have a younger sister. One day, we all drove to a large house in the countryside to collect her. I remember that day as if it were yesterday. At the time, that seemed completely normal to me.

I would have been seven years of age, when Mum and Dad explained I had been adopted. My younger sister Monica was there at the time, although I don't recollect her reaction to what Mum and Dad had said. The social taboos and attitudes towards adoption were conducted in the main as a secret process. It was only during the 1960's that adoption became a subject for open discussion.

This memoir was written many years later, after I immigrated to New Zealand. The central theme is the struggle I experienced in constructing my identity. I needed to know who I was and where I came from. The trauma my sister and I encountered in dealing with our status as adoptees shaped our lives. It was complicated further by Dad suffering from bipolar disorder.

The journey of discovery in search of my birth mother did not start until late in my life. The experience had a profound influence on me, my wife Judy, our two children, my immediate adopted family, their friends and my Irish birth mother and her wider family.

The quest to find your true identity is a process we all experience. My journey to achieve that spans many decades. I was prompted to write the memoir by my wonderful wife Judy to whom I am perpetually grateful. Many friends and family have helped me in compiling the story and I am grateful to them for their support and encouragement. Also, I am indebted to my editors Pam Laird, Erin McKechnie, Richard Aukett and Gretha Benade who made supportive suggestions to develop many aspects of the original draft.

In particular, I am indebted to my son Matthew and Nicola, my daughter, who encouraged me to venture on this journey of discovery. Lastly, I want to sincerely thank my new family in England. You know who you are, there are so many of you to whom I wish to express my gratitude. Thanks also for inviting me into your family and accepting me with so much generosity.

This memoir is a true story. Some names and places have been changed to protect the identity and privacy of those concerned. Paul G. Denny – Auckland, New Zealand, December 12th, 2014

Chapter 1

I have only been back once. We lived in Main Street, which was the first place I called home. My earliest memories go back to 1948. I would have been around three years of age. It's where I first recall thinking about anything. Yet six decades later my recollection of this time and place is still vivid in my mind.

The house that we lived in was Victorian. Built during the middle of the 19th century, it is situated in the village of Sutton Bonington. Eleven miles to the north is Nottingham, a busy and flourishing city in the English East Midlands. Many of the houses in the village date back centuries and the village claims its origins from Anglo-Saxon times. In an earlier era, the village was probably two separate hamlets and after the Norman Conquest, the Doomsday Book of 1086 recorded the villages as "Sudtone" and "Bonitone".

You entered the front door of our house via a covered porch way. I remember the imposing wooden door, painted a glossy jet black. It featured a shiny brass door-knocker, depicting a fearsome lion motif. The door led to a dark central hallway. To the left of the hall was a small lounge and the room to the right was sometimes used for formal dining. The hallway led through to the back of the house, where a good-sized kitchen and scullery featured large windows looking out to the rear garden. Upstairs, a narrow landing led to two large bedrooms at the front, both with wide views of Main Street and the noisy passing traffic. At the rear were two smaller bedrooms and a separate bathroom.

My bedroom was at the back of the house and provided a view over the rear garden. All the upstairs windows were of the sash type. Each frame comprised of two vertical sliding panels. I can still hear Mum's voice continually reminding me to be careful. "Never try and push your bedroom window up, Paul – it's a long drop down to the ground!" Mum and Dad were always so ultra-cautious.

The walls of the house were built from local red brick and the stark white cement pointing broke the blandness of the masonry. On some of the outside walls, dark green shiny ivy clung to the exterior, softening the starkness of the brickwork. The roof was tiled in dark grey slate and was somewhat the worse for its age. I remember that when it rained, Dad would often remark that the small brownish stains on the bedroom ceilings were due to the leaking roof. One day it rained so hard Mum placed a steel bucket under a wet brown stain on my bedroom ceiling to catch the steady drips of rain water. I can still remember the repetitive sound of dripping water hitting the bucket. We never seemed to get soaked, though.

Except for the kitchen and bathroom, all the internal walls displayed dark, stained timber picture rails. In each room a few lonely framed pictures hung on single wire hangers. Predominantly landscapes, they depicted faded images of idyllic country life from another era. As to the furniture and fixtures, my memory only recalls that the house contained sufficient items to provide us with utility with which to live.

What sticks foremost in my mind though are the special memories of my wonderful dog Paddy; my first friend and true companion. He was an Old English sheepdog with long, shaggy grey and white hair which covered his face, making it near impossible to see his dark black eyes or to read what he was attempting to imply. Paddy always wanted to lick my face, which I really enjoyed. Mum and Dad used to say dogs shouldn't be allowed to lick people. Paddy and I didn't agree!

Dad used to leave early in the morning by car to work in Nottingham. After breakfast, which I always ate in the kitchen, Mum would often listen to the radio, tuned to the BBC Light programme. The programmes I remember were *Mrs Dale's Diary,* a new radio sitcom. The rest of the programmes she enjoyed were mainly light music and I grew to accept the continuous broadcasts as being part of daily life. When Dad was in the house, he rarely showed any interest in the radio. When he returned from work each evening, his preference for relaxation was to catch up on local and world events by reading the *Daily Telegraph* newspaper. His prime passion was his addiction to the cryptic crossword.

For the most part, I remember playing by myself. I didn't have any friends as such. Yet, I was contented at the time as I knew no other life. We lived within a very large garden – or so it seemed at the time - containing numerous shady shrubs and a variety of fruit trees. Dad was an avid gardener and took advantage of the good soil and space to grow a wide range of vegetables. Encouraged by wartime rhetoric, "Dig for Victory," his manual labour supplemented the dining table with fresh fruit and vegetables.

The garden at the rear contained a central lawn area, surrounded by mixed flowerbeds, extending to the boundary fence. When the sun was shining, shade was provided by six or eight full grown apple and pear trees, planted throughout the grounds. A large bushy Laburnum tree stood in the left hand corner of the rear garden. The tree was over five metres in height. In springtime, its bright yellow pea-shaped flowers extended like golden rain. Yet, with all its attractiveness, I received severe parental warnings: 'Paul – never touch the tree or its flowers – it will make you poorly!'

Adjacent to the Laburnum were white and mauve flowered lilac trees, extending across the rear boundary. All of them were mature, providing privacy from the adjoining property at the rear. In springtime, the white lilac produced flowers extending dense upright heads, each distinctly isolated within the tree's spreading canopy. Creamy buds developed into a cascade of white flowers, bursting forth with fragrant petals. The side boundaries at the rear had wooden fencing, with brown creosote palings, providing privacy and quiet enjoyment.

Situated at the end of the driveway, down the left-hand side of the house, a large double garage was built against the left-hand boundary. Constructed from timber frames with a rusted, corrugated iron roof, the weatherboard walls were creosoted black and contained small windows facing the lawn. Small, dusty cobwebs hung in delicate veils carelessly over the opaque glass. As Dad kept his car usually in the driveway, the garage became a play area for me as well as providing storage for garden implements and unused pieces of old furniture.

The garage was my refuge, as was the garden, which at the time created my world view. Paddy would often follow me around the garden, or lie asleep on the garage floor as I played with various toys. I recall often playing with a child-size wooden wheelbarrow. I would incessantly fill it with soil, dug from different flower beds. Once the small barrow was loaded, I tipped the soil in another location. Paddy just loved this process. He would follow me behind the barrow, wagging his tail furiously, as I went about loading and tipping the next load of soil. Paddy would join me in this process; his front paws feverishly scooping up the earth at each place I stopped.

Save for my exploits with the wheelbarrow, the garden was well maintained. For a young boy, the landscape of the garden with its wide range of trees, plants and shrubs provided my imagination with the key elements, which over time shaped my notion of the quintessential English country garden.

Mum and Dad moved from Nottingham to Sutton Bonington in 1942. Most large cities then were subject to aerial bombing from Germany. Mum and Dad though continued to work in the city throughout the war years. At the time, Dad would have been 33 and Mum was 30. Mum worked as a dancing teacher during the day and also worked part-time, driving ambulances for the Civil Defence. It was while she was driving ambulances that she met my Dad. Mum was originally from Lincolnshire and her immediate family had moved to Nottingham when she was a young girl. She had a brother, but I never met him or heard much about his life; in later years I always thought it strange.

Dad worked for a London-based company, engaged in the insurance business. He managed their Nottingham branch, having moved from south London in 1939 prior to the outbreak of the war. He only ever worked for one company throughout his working career, starting as an articled clerk after leaving high school. Dad's father had been a saddle and harness maker, who died in a mental asylum. His death by syphilis always haunted him. Dad was only two years old when his father died, so he never really knew him. As I grew up, Dad told me he had no brothers or sisters; when I was thirteen, I discovered this was not true.

Mum and Dad married on Valentine's Day 1942. He started to write a diary which I gained access to many years later, providing me an insight to Mum and Dad's mutual aspirations to have children. They had sought advice from doctors, but to no avail. It seemed by their third wedding anniversary they were reconciled to accept that their ambition to have children of their own was not going to happen.

Many years later, when researching his diaries, I found a cut-out he had pasted of an advertisement in the local paper during late autumn, 1944. Published by the National Children's Adoption Association, it appealed to Catholic adopters seeking Catholic children. The tone of the text amplified the rhetoric of the times: "The Association has now on its books, ten Catholic boy babies of various ages and social backgrounds. Each case has been carefully investigated and adoption decided on only, what we believe, are right and proper grounds. Health sheets are endorsed by doctors and lovely children are now waiting for Catholic parents to come forward, while such attractive months of their lives pass by."[1] Looking back from a modern perspective, the tone and style of the text translates as condescending and verging on romanticism.

***

In England, closed adoption was the normal practice. The process was facilitated in the main by social agencies, which acted as intermediaries on a covert basis, acting between the birth mother and the adoptive parents. Social norms prevalent within many Western cultures reinforced the idea of the family being only constructed biologically within a heterosexual relationship. Adoption was perceived as unacceptable social behaviour and often tainted with social stigma.[2]

Mum and Dad's desire for a family was realised in early 1946, when they adopted me. I was born in

---

[1] Mary Ellison, National Children Adoption Association, Catholic Herald, 1944.

[2] Karen March. "Perception of Adoption as Social Stigma: Motivation for Search and Reunion." *Journal of Marriage and the Family*, no 57 (August 1995): p. 654.

Hampshire in December 1945 and my name was Richard. After my legal adoption, I was given a new name; Mum and Dad called me Paul and when I was three months old, they collected me from a children's home in Northampton and brought me back to Sutton Bonington.

Although I have no recollection of those early years, I settled in with Mum and Dad, bonding with them as time progressed. I do remember when I was two, receiving a Christmas present from my parents. It was a toy car made from pressed steel, with four shiny wheels and thin rubber tyres. Painted light blue, with dark blue stripes along each side, I enjoyed peddling the car around the lawn. As you might guess, my car lived in the garage after I'd finished playing with it. Paddy followed me as I peddled my car around the garden. When he got tired, Paddy always retired to sleep in his favourite sunny spot; next to the outside kitchen door, immediately below my bedroom window.

Not many people visited our house in Main Street. I was only two years old and my first recollection of a regular visitor was the fishmonger Mr Chudleigh, who came to our house every Friday. A large, jovial man with a ruddy face and untidy grey hair, he wore a dark blue and white striped apron. It covered the front of his chest and brown trousers, down to his large black shoes. A white shirt with sleeves turned up, exhibited two strong hairy arms and large rough hands.

His dark blue van had large chrome plated headlamps. At the back were two hinged doors with high circular windows. When he opened the rear doors, on the floor inside were metal ice trays containing fresh fish. Mum's favourite was yellow smoked haddock. Sometimes Mr Chudleigh would ask me if I liked winkles. I always smiled, replying, 'Yes please.' Then he'd scoop up a full paper carton of shiny black winkles, beaming broadly. After he had left, Mum picked our way through the tasty

19

shell fish with a large pin, even though they reminded me of snails I'd seen in the garden.

In December 1948, I turned three. The occasion is as clear to me now as it was on that day. I'd been happily playing by myself in the back garden, well wrapped up against the cold weather in a blue coat. Underneath I wore grey dungarees and muddy Wellington boots. Mum opened the kitchen door and although I don't recollect her actual words, it went something like: 'Paul, come inside, it's your lunch time!'

I didn't feel hungry so I walked out of earshot, heading to the back of the garden. Even at such a young age, I often hid from Mum and Dad. It made me feel safe and secure.

It must have been less than a minute when Mum opened the door again.

Speaking more loudly this time, she called out, 'Paul – I've asked you once. Come in for your lunch, I've something important to tell you!'

I walked back slowly from the rear of the garden towards the kitchen door.

'Can't I come in later Mum, please? I'm not hungry yet!'

'No Paul – come inside straight away! The food will get cold!'

I conceded: my curiosity exceeded my appetite. I climbed a wooden stool at the kitchen table and sat down. I waited for Mum to bring the soup tureen to the table. Paddy lay down beside me hoping for a titbit; he usually enjoyed licking the soup bowls clean after the meal.

'What's the soup Mum?'

'Minestrone – your favourite!'

She lifted the lid of the tureen. Filling a large ladle she filled both bowls with soup. I just loved steaming minestrone soup.

'Paul, would you like some bread?'

'Yes please Mum. Can I have some butter too?' She buttered two slices of bread placing each slice on our side plates.

'The soup is very hot, be careful.'

I'd already half-filled my spoon, blowing carefully into the soup.

'Mum, what were you going to tell me?' I said, looking down and slowly tasting the steaming soup.

'I think we'll discuss it when your dad is home from work,' she said. 'Tomorrow's Saturday, so we can talk about it then! I should have thought about it more carefully. I'm sorry Paul.'

I recall my response. 'Oh please Mum, you promised!'

Mum dropped the subject, as if she had never mentioned telling me something important. After a few minutes silence, she asked, 'Paul, would you like some more soup? Let me fill your bowl and butter you another slice of bread.'

I replied, 'Thanks Mum.' She passed me the bread, her demeanour and tone of voice had changed. The topic was not open for further discussion. I didn't dare ask her again and waited for Saturday to arrive. I remember clearly how angry Mum and Dad looked at me when they didn't want to discuss an issue any further. Mum's response to a question from me when I asked '*Why*' would be to smile back and just say '*Z.*'

On most weekday afternoons, Mum and I walked to the local village shops. It took no more than a few minutes, although for me, it felt like ages. The village was large enough to have a number of shops, including a post office and general store. The shop I enjoyed most was Leyton's. It had bold blue and gold signage above the windows, proudly displaying the retailer's name. I couldn't read the sign, Frank Leyton & Sons – Grocer & Provisions, but I knew the name Leyton's by heart. The store had always caught my attention; the aroma of food, the bustle of shoppers and the boisterous activity that took place fascinated me.

Leyton's was a family business. It was a hive of industrious activity, possessing a range of intriguing machines for slicing bacon, to cutting large pieces of cheese. My favourite was the cheese wire cutter. The person cutting the cheese held a stretched wire, secured to a white marble cutting bench. By applying downwards pressure with the wire over the cheese it cut easily through the block. It just seemed like magic to me.

Saturday turned out to be sunny and Dad was in the garden. Paddy was asleep and I was out playing with my pride and joy, my blue car, and generally poking my nose into anything that fascinated me. I was anxious to find out what Mum had wanted to tell me the day before. I drove over to the vegetable patch where Dad was working. He wore long brown trousers and a brown and white striped shirt with the sleeves rolled up. His gardening shoes were old and crusty. On his wrist, he wore a gold watch that reflected the sun's rays as he dug into the potato patch. Using a garden fork to lift each clump, he shook every forkful robustly, separating the leaves and clinging soil from the crop.

'Laddie, you can help me if you like,' he said casually. He moved the shallow oval trug along the ridge of potatoes. I liked Dad calling me Laddie; it made me feel that I belonged.

'What shall I do?' I asked, looking up towards his shaded face. He was wearing his well-worn gardening Panama, constructed from light coloured straw. The wide brim shaded his face.

'Please go and ask your mum if she wants some potatoes and beans for lunch?'

I peddled my car back towards the house and returned a few minutes later. 'Mum wants both,' I said to Dad, who by now had already placed some potatoes in the wooden trug.

'Can I pick the beans?' I said.

'Yes Laddie – Of course you can,' he said, pointing me towards the row of runner beans, entwined on thin bamboo canes.

Dad and I quickly completed our task, filling the small trug to the brim.

'Let's go inside, Laddie. Mum needs the vegetables for lunch.'

As we entered the kitchen, I could smell the roast lamb cooking and the succulent aroma made me feel hungry. I sat down and watched.

Dad placed the vegetables in the kitchen sink.

'I'll peel the potatoes, dear,' he said to mum. 'You sit down and relax.'

'Thanks darling,' she said. 'I expect you're both hungry?'

'I'm starving!' I replied.

'Me too,' said Dad.

Dad finished peeling the potatoes; placing them in a cream enamel saucepan filled with water. Carefully he placed the saucepan on the hob.

'The meat should be cooked in about thirty minutes,' Mum said to Dad.

'That's good,' he said as he started to splice and string the beans. After he had finished, he placed them in a similar saucepan. Covering them with water, he placed them next to the potatoes. Turning on the gas, he struck a match and lit both gas rings.

After the vegetables were cooked, Mum got up from her chair.

'I'll drain the vegetables, dear,' Dad said, as Mum opened the oven door. She placed the hot baking tray containing the lamb on the kitchen bench.

Dad lifted the meat from the steel tray, placing the meat on an oval carving plate. He then proceeded to make the gravy. Adding cornflower and water to the rich dark juices from the cooked lamb, he stirred the mix and poured it into a glass gravy boat. 'Yummy,' I said to Mum and Dad. 'It smells really good!'

After we had finished our main course, Mum produced a homemade apple tart with vanilla flavoured custard - always one of my favourites!

'Do you want a drink of tea, Paul?' Mum asked, after we had finished our meal. Tea was very much a tradition in our household and I remember clearly both Mum and Dad always drinking copious amounts at any opportunity. I quickly acquired the habit.

'Yes please, Mum,' I replied. Dad gestured towards Mum, indicating we should all go into the garden to drink our tea.

Immediately outside the kitchen door was a small terrace paved with creamy coloured bricks. Two sides of the patio contained a small rockery, providing ample room for four chairs plus a sturdy rustic table, all of which were painted dark green. Once seated, Mum poured two large cups of tea and a small white and blue-rimmed mug for me.

Nobody spoke for a few minutes. Mum offered us both a ginger biscuit. Dad declined and I bit my biscuit. I think my father spoke first. Before speaking, he refilled his pipe with fresh tobacco and lit it.

As he drew his pipe away from his mouth, he placed it slowly down on the garden table.

'Laddie – Mum and I have some wonderful news,' he said, looking towards me. 'In a few weeks, we're going to have a daughter. She'll be your sister.'

I didn't know what to say. Mum then turned towards me.

'Dad and I are so excited. We hope to pick her up in a few months' time.'

Mum and Dad had never spoken about having another child, but I knew from their tone of voice it was very important to them. To me at nearly three, the whole idea seemed to be completely normal. I had no idea where babies came from, let alone what the process of adoption was. I just accepted the idea and didn't give it much further thought. Mum said we would pick her up together in a few months' time.

The topic did not come up again until the summer of 1949, when I was reaching my fourth birthday. I don't remember being curious about having a younger sister. In hindsight, Mum and Dad must have talked about the proposition between themselves. When they had first told me about my sister, they did not know who she was or when the young girl they planned to adopt would be available. All I understood was I would have a sister to play with within a few months. It sounded a good idea and Mum and Dad were enthusiastic. I didn't mention it again.

***

Every Sunday we went to church by car. The journey took less than half an hour. I always enjoyed travelling in our black Wolsey 10. The smell of brown leather upholstery and the sound of the engine throbbing blended with family chatter. In summer, warm air pumped out from the heater unit, which Dad said he had asked the garage mechanic to fix many times. Dad sometimes let me sit in the front seat next to him. Not being tall enough, I couldn't see much outside.

We always arrived early for Mass and I soon figured out that it was to be certain of a seat. In addition, Dad was a stickler for being on time, not just for going to church, but on any occasion. Inside the church, the familiar smell of burning candles and the lingering aroma of sweet-burning incense always filled the air. The three altars had several statues with vases of fresh flowers at their base. Hanging in front of the main altar was a glowing red glass sanctuary lamp. My introduction to Catholicism and its rituals stemmed from my earliest days.

The long days of summer shortened. In December I would be four, the days and nights became colder and we spent most time indoors. The excitement of Christmas was approaching fast. One afternoon, I remember Dad and Mum taking me for a walk. We brought back small holly branches from the bare winter hedgerows and searched unsuccessfully for mistletoe.

The holly leaves were dark green and glossy and each leaf had spiky serrations along the edges. Below some of the green foliage were small, bright, red berries. Dad entwined the holly stems on wire frames and hung some off picture rails around the house. Other decorations were simple wreaths, some with white or red candles tied with bows of red and gold satin. Wherever there was free space, Dad found a space to fill. The largest wreath I remember hung outside on our shiny black front door.

Pride of place was our Christmas tree, which was erected in the front lounge. Dad transplanted the tree from our garden annually, returning it to the ground on twelfth night. The container was covered in brightly coloured red paper, placed within a large terracotta pot. The tree stood in the corner of the room and Mum left the curtains open, so people walking down the street could see the lights. Set amongst the pine's small branches were bright reflecting chains of silver and gold tinsel. They dangled with coloured glass spheres hanging from the bows, enhanced by multitudes of coloured fairy lights. Nestled below the tree was a nativity crib. Made from cardboard, fine sawdust and shredded straw were sprinkled on the floor. Before going to bed, I remember sitting and watching the glimmering tree and the silver star at its peak in silhouette against the dark night sky outside.

Christmas decorations extended to the lounge and dining room, embellished with a labyrinth of crisscrossed handmade paper chains. In the lounge, Dad strung a string cord across one wall, secured at each end to the picture rail. Attached were brightly coloured cards from friends and relatives. On Christmas Eve, Dad re-lit a half-burnt log, stored from last year's Yuletide festival.

The Christmas of 1949 was unseasonably mild. Shortly after New Year, the weather turned bitterly cold. Sadly, Paddy, my best mate, became very ill. For me it was a wakeup call because I had never seen an animal sick before. Dad took Paddy to the local vet and I found out later he had contracted distemper, an incurable disease. When Dad returned from visiting the vet, Paddy was not with him. I asked him what the matter was. I could tell from looking at Dad's face that something was terribly wrong.

'I am so sorry Laddie – Paddy was very sick and the vet thought it best to put him to sleep. He's not in pain any more. Mum and I are so very sorry.'

Dad picked me up in his arms, hugging me close. I began to cry. I must have known as he held me closely, things were never going to be the same again.

'Dad,' I said with tears streaming down my face. 'Paddy's not coming back home ever again, is he?'

'No Laddie – sadly for us all, he won't be coming home again.'

That night I recall still crying when I went to bed, knowing Paddy would never come back. This was my first experience of death and personal loss. I still have a small black and white photograph of Paddy. His departure from my world took ages for me to accept. The memories of his friendly face, his bright black eyes mostly hidden behind his straggly unkempt coat, remain with me forever. I began to wonder what, if anything, would ever replace my best friend. Mum and Dad promised I would have another dog but from my perspective, I was unable to visualise that ever happening. Life did go on for all of us and time helped the healing process, until one day in late spring 1950, when all our lives changed forever.

***

It must have been a weekend, because Dad was at home. I remember the telephone ringing loudly in the hallway. Mum had taken the call. After the call ended, she returned to the kitchen, her face beaming with excitement. Dad was reading me a story from one of my favourite books and he turned towards Mum.

'Who was that on the telephone darling?' he asked, placing the book to one side.

'It was the Catholic children's home at Colston Bassett, darling!' she said, as Dad rose from his chair. Moving towards Mum, I watched him embrace her closely.

'They have found a daughter for us. I just can't believe it, I'm just so happy!' she said.

After a short pause, Dad looked over to me.

'Paul – this is wonderful news! Mum and Dad are so thrilled. You're going to have a little sister.' He turned again towards Mum giving her a gentle hug.

Reflecting back, I can't recall precisely how I felt. Mum and Dad continued to explain we would all be going together in the car the following weekend to meet her. They told me they were going to call her Monica, although many years later, I discovered her birth parents had given her another name.

The next weekend Dad drove us to Colston Bassett, a small village to the east of Sutton Bonington. The journey took less than an hour and this time I sat in the back seat. Mum and Dad were busy talking and I looked up and saw the stark shapes of countless bare trees and leafless hedgerows, slipping past my side window. We arrived in the village before lunch and the weather was still bitterly cold. The cloudless sky was blue and although the sun shone brightly, it extended little warmth. Dad said the children's home had previously been a private country estate and the building we were seeking was Colston Bassett Hall. Dad found the Hall soon enough, located a short distance from the centre of the village.

Colston Bassett Hall sits well back from the road, surrounded by lush green parkland. The spacious fields within the park were scattered with large oak trees, most of which were securely anchored, but some had fallen and were decaying on the ground. As we drove past the perimeter of the estate, grazing sheep occupied the visible pasture. The animals were feeding eagerly on the winter grass, while black carrion crows surveyed the grounds from high up in the trees.

The Hall dates from around 1704, although a property had been on the site from the middle ages. The mansion's architectural style is Palladian and its imposing setting reflects the splendour of the estate. In 1949, the owner of the property, Sir Edward Le Marchant, sold the Hall to the Nottingham Catholic Children's Society and it became a maternity home and a refuge for children available for adoption.[3]

We approached the Hall, entering through a large white stone gateway. The meandering driveway, leading from the road was fenced on both sides with rusty black cast iron fencing. As we drove through the fertile green pastures of the park, the Hall came into view in the distance. The driveway led up on to a large gravel forecourt, adjacent to the Hall's frontage.

We left the Wolsey and climbed the stone-flagged steps leading up towards the entrance. I followed Mum and Dad as we entered an open double doorway, leading into a large, high roofed entrance hall. As we entered, I recall clearly seeing a tall nun, dressed in black and wearing a white veil. After entering the reception area, she welcomed Mum and Dad. Then she smiled at me.

Within a few minutes an older stout nun, arrived in the reception area. She introduced herself as the Mother Superior. Her stiff manner frightened me. She turned towards Mum and Dad, suggesting I might like to see more of Colston Bassett Hall. She took my hand and introduced me to the tall nun who had met us as we arrived.

'Paul, Sister Frances will show you around the Hall,' said the Mother Superior. 'I hope you enjoy looking around. Your mum and dad have to sort some paperwork out with me.'

Before I could say anything, Sister Frances smiled and took my hand. I wanted Mum to come with me but I was too scared to ask.

---

[3] Colston Bassett Local History Group. Colston Bassett Hall, retrieved on 19th Nov 2013 from
http://www.colstonbassetthistory.org.uk/readarticle.php?article_id=17

'Mum and I will be waiting here when you get back,' Dad said, reassuringly, holding Mum's hand. 'We'll see you soon, Laddie!'

'Come along, Paul,' said Sister Francis with a broad smile. I smiled back obediently and waved goodbye. She continued holding my hand firmly. Sister Frances confirmed I would soon be back again with Mum and Dad. I felt reassured, but inside I really wanted to stay with Mum and Dad and meet my new sister. It felt somehow they wanted to get rid of me but I was too frightened to ask why.

As we walked along a wide corridor, I heard the jangling of beads rubbing against the nun's stark black habit. Around her waist, her leather waistband displayed a rosary of brown inter-linking beads. They hung down her right thigh, displaying at the end, a shiny metal crucifix. It seemed quite scary to me, but I wasn't really afraid.

The floor of the walkway was paved with black and white stone tiles. Our footsteps resonated with the jangling from her rosary beads. Ahead of us was an enclosed central plaza with a high glass roof and around the internal walls were large double doors, painted black. Each door had a shiny black handle. We stopped outside a door at the far end of the plaza.

Sister Frances opened the door. I followed her into a large cream room with windows looking out onto the park. The room was light with sunshine and contained children's cots with their backs all turned against the walls. Two women dressed in white uniforms were looking after young babies. One spoke and smiled when we entered.

'Good morning, Sister Frances. Who's the young man you have brought with you today?'

'This is Paul, I am showing him around the Hall,' she replied.

Sister Frances then ushered me towards one of the cots. As I stared through the slats she said, 'Paul, these are some of the babies waiting for a new home!'

While some babies were crying, many appeared to be sleeping. Looking up at Sister Frances I asked her which baby was my sister. She replied in a soft voice, 'You'll meet her shortly.' I felt scared, thinking Mum and Dad may leave me behind and take my new sister home with them, instead of me.

We left the nursery after saying goodbye to the two women. As we walked back along the chequered tiled corridor, I kept thinking my sister must be somewhere else. In my mind, I kept thinking, where had all the babies' mothers and fathers gone? It all seemed so very strange and it made me feel so sad.

When we got back, Sister Frances knocked on the annex room door.

'Come in,' said Mother Superior.

I followed Sister Frances into the room. 'Paul, I'll leave you now with your mum and dad,' she said.

Mother Superior looked at me, barely smiling from behind her desk. 'Paul, please sit down with your Mum and Dad.'

Sister Frances said goodbye and left. Seated in front of a large desk were mum and dad, with pens in their hands. They were writing on documents laid out on the desk. I started to climb a chair next to dad. He laid down his pen and lifted me up into his arms.

'Mum and I have just finished, Laddie!' he said. 'How was the tour of the Hall?'

'I saw lots of babies in a big room. Sister Frances said my new sister would be with you! Where is she?'

Mum turned and Dad, passed me across to Mum, who lifted me onto her lap. Trying to reassure me, she said, 'Paul, Monica will be with us in a few minutes.'

Before I had a chance to respond, the door leading into the office opened. I can still see in my mind's eye a nun holding the hand of a small young girl. Dressed in a pink dress with a smocked bodice, she wore long white socks and black shoes. Her short hair was parted at the centre and two ponytails were held together tightly by rubber bands.

Dad stood up and looked at her face. 'Hello Monica,' he said with a warm smile. 'Sister told me you are a big girl now and your second birthday was in February.'

Monica looked back nervously at mum and dad and then at me.

'Hello,' I said, trying to smile through my bewilderment. I had expected Monica to be a tiny baby, like the ones in the nursery. When she did not reply, I was disappointed.

I moved away from mum. Dad took my hand as Mum picked up Monica. It all happened very quickly. Mother Superior said goodbye, and Mum and Dad ushered Monica and me towards the door. We all walked slowly out into the hallway, entered the car park and headed towards the Wolsey.

Reflecting back to that day, the process must have been incredibly distressing for Monica, as well as me. Obviously, Mum and Dad would have known Monica was two years old. They had never said to me that she would not be a small baby. My previous expectations of having a baby sister were unfulfilled. For Monica, the transition from an institution to new parents with a four-year-old boy would have been bewildering, and I too was at a loss to comprehend the dynamics of the situation.

After the nuns had waved us goodbye, we drove down the driveway. I sat in the rear seat with Monica at my side.

That was the last time I ever visited Colston Basset Hall, until recently. When I did, I felt cold inside, reflecting back on that bleak unhappy day.

That encounter should have been warm and joyful. The process we all endured that day sounds unbelievable. Yet, it reflected the *zeitgeist*, in particular the practice of closed adoption, where dark secrets were concealed covertly and the stiff upper lip promoted by the establishment was the order of the day.

I never discovered whether Monica had come directly from her birth mother, or whether she had been given up for adoption at birth. For me, the experience of our first meeting proved later to be the beginning of a traumatised relationship with my new sister. I did not speak to Monica during the short journey back to Sutton Bonington; neither of us exchanged a word. As Dad drove, both Mum and Dad attempted to talk with Monica, but the process of engagement proved difficult. I discovered many years later how Monica suppressed her trauma, visibly evident from our first encounter and how it would affect her future happiness and sense of identity. Eventually the consequences would unfold tragically over all our lives.

***

Springtime 1950 moved quickly towards the long lazy days of summer. Monica and I went about each day, as children normally attempt to do. Yet, the just over two-year difference in our ages frustrated our ability to connect as siblings. We sometimes played together in the house and the traditional amusements of young boys competed with the arrival of dolls. I recall some were made from cut-out cardboard figures with paper clothes to match. During that summer, I spent most of my time playing in the garden, while Monica preferred spending her time with Mum.

When I look back on old photographs taken by Dad with his Kodak Brownie, they show Monica and me playing alone separated in the garden. In photographs, we were seldom pictured together as a family group. The black and white images capture us as individuals, not as part of a dynamic family unit but in isolation. Monica and I unconsciously accepted this practice as the framework of our relationship. It prevented us both from experiencing the love and friendship we needed, to form our own unique identity and create a bond of love between us.

Dad referred to Monica as Motty; a term of endearment. It seemed a normal gesture to me. I was used to him calling me, Laddie. Looking back, for Monica, terms of endearment, although well intentioned by Dad, may well have caused her difficulty in constructing her own identity. Monica was the adopted name chosen by Mum and Dad. She had a previous Christian name, which to this date I have never been privy. To my mind the name Motty as a form of endearment, may have complicated her sense of identity although I shall never really know for sure.

One sultry day, during the late summer of 1950, the family were out enjoying a brisk walk in the countryside. We left the house mid-morning and Dad helped prepare the picnic. Mum wrapped the sandwiches in greaseproof paper, followed by four hard-boiled eggs, placing them in a brown woven picnic basket. Before closing the lid, Mum added a thermos flask of tea and some fresh fruit supplied by Leyton's.

We set out from Main Street and within a few minutes, we were in the heart of the countryside. Mum was holding Monica's hand and Dad and I walked in front. We walked for a while and soon I began feeling tired. As we ambled down the winding lane, Mum and Dad chose an ideal spot to rest. We entered an empty grass field through a wide five-bar wooden gate and settled in the shade from the mid-morning sun under a large chestnut tree, standing beside a thick wild hedgerow.

The sweet smell of freshly cut grass enhanced my senses. The hot midday sun would soon dry out the freshly cut grass to become winter hay. Dad opened up a large groundsheet and I remember the tranquil silence as we sat admiring the view. I soon wanted to explore the high hedgerow next to our picnic spot, searching for discarded springtime bird nests. I hadn't walked more than a few yards, when Mum beckoned me back for lunch. As we ate, we chatted amongst ourselves. It was no less than light innocuous banter, which siblings and their parents might normally exchange.

I remember Dad speaking first. His voice seemed more serious in tone than usual. Monica and I sharpened our attention; he told us we would all be leaving Sutton Bonington in a few weeks. He had accepted a new job in a country town, close to the sea. Moving to a new house, in a new town had never entered my imagination. Monica, I recall, expressed no reaction at all.

Mum followed up optimistically on Dad's news, saying we would be able to travel easily and explore the local countryside. The many seaside resorts scattered along the Devonshire coastline would also be a new experience for all of us. The idea of moving was daunting, but I began to accept that change would provide new pastimes, and perhaps the chance to make some friends. We were going to live close to the sea so Mum said I could learn to swim. As the day went on, the idea of moving began to slowly gain acceptance. Like most young impressionable children, we accepted the notion of change with little hesitation.

That night, after Mum had turned out my bedside lamp, I began to think more about our day in the countryside. Mum and Dad had told us we would arrive in Exeter by late summer. By the end of that year, I would be five years old and would start my first school a few months later in the spring of 1951. Of course, I had no idea what school really meant and what I would experience. Nevertheless, the idea of change appealed to my natural sense of optimism.

One topic continually going through my mind was. Monica had come from a children's home, where did I come from! I would find out more after moving to Exeter.

Chapter 2

In England good weather in September is often called an Indian summer. This September was no exception. We left Sutton Bonington and travelled by car to Exeter and I have no recollection of the journey. I do remember clearly my first sighting of our new home. It was very different to what I had expected; I had naively assumed it would be similar to the property we had vacated. Our old house was a detached cottage, in a small village; our new home was in a street of identical suburban semi-detached houses. Located in a quiet street, there were small trees planted along the grass verge, between the road and the footpath. To me they looked like weary sentries.

In comparison the house seemed very small. When it was furnished with our possessions though, it soon began to feel like home. On the ground floor, adjacent to the front bay window, was the front entrance, protected by a small covered porch. The door led into a narrow hallway, covered in dark green carpet. An oak wooden coat stand stood against the wall, its round mirror too high for me to reach. The base contained a steel stand for Dad's favourite walking sticks, as well as two large black umbrellas. All our raincoats lived hanging on the stand and the smell of damp coats always permeated the hall space.

To the left, a small lounge looked out on to the roadway. Inside, a light brown tiled fireplace dominated the room. In the centre of the mantelpiece was a brass carriage clock and on either side were brass candlesticks. Over the fireplace was an octagonal mirror, hanging from a chain and to the right, were two wooden shelves painted cream. The top shelf had an imposing Murphy radio, encased in dark chocolate Bakelite. It took pride of place, surrounded by ceramic and coloured glass ornaments. There were family photographs; one of Monica and me looking away from each other and smiling faintly. Below the lower shelf was a row of publications; mostly well used hardbacks. Centred in front of the books, was Dad's mahogany pipe rack. The six, well used pipes retained the putrid smell of spent tobacco.

A small settee and two small armchairs filled the central space, and in the recess of the bay, was a polished oak gate-legged table, which once belonged to Mum's grandmother. In the centre of the room was a low circular occasional table, containing a large blue glass ashtray. Above, hanging from the white ceiling, a shaded central light emitted insufficient radiance with which to read. Between the armchairs though, stood a wooden standard lamp, its thin, wide gossamer shade emitting adequate light with which to read by.

The dining room faced out towards the rear garden. Plum red velvet curtains were drawn across at night. In the centre of the room was a light oak dining table with six high-back slatted chairs. The only other furniture was a two-drawer sideboard in dark oak with a matching wooden serving trolley, with polished castor wheels. A blue and yellow Kashmir carpet covered most of the dark, stained wooden floor boards. On the walls were two framed prints from our previous house.

The only other room downstairs was a small kitchen. The walls were painted light sky blue and the only décor on the walls were three white hand painted geese with bright orange beaks, flying in formation. The room had a small alcove, used for washing clothes, containing a Hoover washtub and hand wringer on the side.

Our kitchen was where we ate breakfast and lunch. Below the window was a stainless steel sink bench with fitted cupboards below. To the side was a closed pantry and adjacent was a cream enamel gas cooker with the grill above the hob. The floor was covered in linoleum with a black and white square pattern. A rear door led out on to the driveway, which offered access through to the rear garden.

The staircase from the hallway led up towards a landing area. The first of the six doors led into Mum and Dad's room directly over the lounge below, and had the only bay window upstairs. Three others, led to small bedrooms and the fourth door to a tiny, white tiled bathroom. Next to the bathroom the W.C. had a small opaque window, looking on to the driveway running alongside the property.

Monica's bedroom looked out over the front porch. The room I slept in was at the back of the house. Like Monica's room, it contained a single bed with different coloured bedspreads. The only soft toys I remember, sitting on our beds, were a grotesque black-faced doll on my bed, and on Monica's, a pale ceramic doll dressed in knitted clothes. Each room contained a small wardrobe and chest of drawers. The black stained floors were polished and partly covered with rectangular scatter carpets down either side of our beds. Against the light green walls were small shelves, filled with children's books. In my room was a long painted wooden chest, containing a mélange of toys.

In our home, we were both taught to respect each person's bedrooms; each room was our private domain. I do not remember how Mum and Dad's bedroom was furnished; except to say it was always considered private. I can only recall briefly ever entering their room; the door was always closed and it seemed inappropriate to enter. Likewise, Monica and I rarely gave access to each other's rooms, which sadly exacerbated our isolation from each other.

Compared to our previous house, the gardens were a disappointment. The small rectangular garden at the front comprised a lawn edged with standard roses. The property was separated from the roadway by a low reddish brick wall, with access via a single wrought iron gateway. A narrow concrete pathway led straight towards the front door. The open asphalt driveway was shared with the property next door and led up to adjoining brick garages at the rear.

The back garden had no trees or places to discover. Outside the kitchen door were grimy concrete pavers, separating the house from the lawn. A washing line stretched out between two wooden posts. The only colour in the garden came from pink roses which grew on trellises, mounted on both side fences. The rest of the grounds were given over to a vegetable area, containing a small garden shed. Its gloomy walls were clad in weatherboards and the black bitumen roof was steeply pitched. Inside were garden tools, as well as Dad's orange Qualcast push mower. Mum's old pushbike was stored inside, but I never saw her ride it. In front of the low back fence were a few rows of forlorn raspberry canes, tied to horizontal rusty galvanised wires. Except for winter, the green dense foliage was a place I sometimes used to like to hide.

Our first winter in Exeter was cold. From October until the spring we always had a fire burning in the dining room. Dad filled up the steel coal scuttle every night from the leaky outside concrete coal-bunker. When Dad was working, Mum replenished it, backing-up the burning coal throughout the day. After it rained the coal was damp. Fumes and smoke belched from the fire, assisted by draughts of cold air drawn down the chimney, some of which escaped into the room. Not that coal smoke was the only hazard, although I thought it was fun when the fire misbehaved.

Mum and Dad smoked tobacco. They mainly indulged their habit within the confines of the house. Dad smoked cigarettes during the daytime and in the evening would light up one of his brier pipes from his mahogany pipe rack. Mum smoked Du Maurier tipped cigarettes, packaged in bright red. When they smoked the air was thick with toxins, which often combined with smoke emitted from the coal fire. For Monica and I this was normal. At the time we both thought no more of it. In those days, most adults smoked, as did their children indirectly, and social attitudes towards the habit were non-judgemental. I distinctly remember how the grey smoke discoloured the white ceilings in the house, as well as yellowing the wallpaper, particularly downstairs.

After living in urban suburbia for a few months, our life soon began to feel normal. As we entered the New Year, I began to think much more about my first school. Mum said I would need to have a brand new school uniform. Shortly after Christmas, Mum, Monica and I travelled by bus into the city to purchase the necessary clothing.

Our first port of call was a shoe shop in the centre of Exeter, filled with parents and their children. To determine the shoes were the correct size, your feet were placed into an X-ray machine. In those days, many children's shoe shops had special X-ray equipment on site. I took great delight in looking through the viewing window, observing my toes wiggling inside my new shoes. It seemed like magic; climbing two steps towards the machine and looking downwards at the image below, projected onto a green screen monitor.

My pride and joy was my first school blazer. It was royal blue with white silk braid edging around the collar and lapels. The breast pocket displayed a large embroidered school badge. The rest of the uniform comprised a white shirt, a blue striped tie and light grey short trousers with grey socks to match. To complete the uniform, boys wore a navy blue gabardine rain coat with matching peaked cap. The hat felt special; it had the school motif stitched on the front.

My first day at school commenced in the early spring of 1951 and was my second encounter with Catholic nuns. Dad took me to school in our new Austin A40. The car was painted a conservative dull sky grey. It was very different from the Wolsey. It had no leather seats or wooden facia; instead it was built only for utility. The convent and school had been established in 1896 by a community of French nuns. They established the facility within a complex of buildings known as Palace Gate.[4] The nuns converted part of the compound into a private chapel, completed in 1928. Our school was adjacent to Exeter Cathedral and the grounds contained the Bishops' Palace. To add further ambiance to the location, the remains of the city wall, constructed during the Roman occupation of Britain, was visible from within our school grounds.

When we arrived at school, Dad handed me over to the care of one of the nuns and I joined a group of other newly enrolled children. After we had assembled, we were all led up a steep flight of stairs. At the top, we encountered two wide open doors leading into a small chapel. Inside the church, on both sides of the aisle, were rows of graceful wooden pews.

Each boy and girl was ushered towards a vacant seat.

The floor was covered with a mosaic of polished wooden parquetry, laid out in a herringbone pattern. The high ceiling of the nave was broken by three wide semi-circular arches, each strung between opposing windows. On

---

[4] Jean Thompson, "Exeter Memories," *A Night to Remember*, retrieved on 12th Dec 2013 from
http://www.exetermemories.co.uk/em/_story/story_135.php

either side of the nave were four large glass windows in rectangular steel frames. In the centre of each, was a circular, opaque glass panel in bright yellow glass.

Looking down towards the altar, the sanctuary floor shone with polished tiles of blue, green and white marble. In the centre was a white marble altar, surrounded by a circular scarlet carpet. A marble tabernacle with shiny brass doors was set between two lacquered candle sticks. Behind the altar were three narrow, vertical stained windows, depicting images of saints.

The chapel had a memorable smell; sweet incense and burning candles, the fragrance of Sunday Mass. The only other memory was the familiar scent of fresh wax polish that reminded me of home. The ambiance of the chapel conveyed to those sitting, the sound of silence. A gentle calm was only broken by the slight movement of restless young children and their teachers.

When we had all settled quietly, our anticipation was rewarded. Standing at the front, the Mother Superior greeted us with words of welcome and sternly told us we would attend Mass three times a week. None of the children spoke a word. She then proceeded to call out each of our names, asking us to leave the chapel and reassemble outside the entrance doors. There we would be met and segregated again by our individual class teacher.

After joining my new classmates, I looked more closely at my teacher, a short rotund woman wearing a black habit. On her head she wore a black veil. Her long flowing gown had full-length sleeves and was drawn in at the waist by a thin leather belt. Attached to it was a string of black rosary beads, dangling. Her face was partly obscured by small shiny round steel spectacles and her eyes moved quickly from child to child with piercing intensity.

'My name is Sister Patricia,' she announced in a loud voice. 'Children, please follow me to your classroom, and no talking!'

We all duly complied with her command and climbed down the stairs together, the only sound was of many tiny feet in new black shoes. Sister Patricia led us along a dingy corridor, leading eventually to a large wooden door. Opening it wide, we all followed her into a small classroom. In front of us a wide charcoal grey chalkboard dominated the wall.

'Will you all please take a seat,' she said, in an uncompromising voice. Without exception we scrambled to find a seat among the rows of long wooden benches. The most popular place to sit, I found out later, was at the back of the classroom. I was lucky; I secured a seat in the corner of the back row.

The room was lit by four large bulbs hanging down from long black cables, screened by circular dark-green enamel steel shades. Our teacher was enthroned on a rectangular wooden plinth in a corner at the front of the class. Mounted in the centre, was a tall mahogany writing desk facing towards the class. When Sister Patricia was seated, most children were unable to see clearly whether she could see us or not.

Every school day began with students gathering in the downstairs assembly hall. Mother Superior would invariably make a welcome address, swiftly followed by a collective dismissal. Children whose roster was to attend Mass in the chapel would leave the hall and climb the stairs to find a pew as far back from the front as possible. Those remaining would walk to their individual classrooms and patiently await the entrance of their class teacher.

Sister Patricia excelled at providing an environment focused on rote learning. Our lessons centred on calligraphy, basic arithmetic and reading. Every day we received religious instruction, constructed around Bible stories. Writing was mastered by copying lettering from the blackboard. We transcribed lettering and numbers in pencil, attempting to emulate our teacher's precise copperplate script in chalk, into our own lined writing books. Each day, by following a process of rotation, Sister Patricia instructed us to read aloud a short passage from our reading books.

I found school tedious. One day I was daydreaming, gazing out of the classroom window. The familiar view was a constant distraction and the large oval lawn, surrounded by a backdrop of hefty yew trees was more compelling than schoolwork. The lawn was surrounded by a grey asphalt pathway and the grounds were used by students during playtime breaks.

The area provided the only feasible opportunity for any social interaction. Conversation between children during class was discouraged and for the most part forbidden. Most children attending school brought a lunch of cut sandwiches, often accompanied by an apple or a small chocolate bar. One morning my lazy mind had drifted more towards satisfying my appetite than concentrating on Sister Patricia's scholastic utterances.

Discipline within the classroom was maintained by a regime based on fear and punishment. Talking in class time, when not directly addressing the teacher, would be punished by either banishment to a corner of the classroom, or being caned publicly in front of the whole class.

That day my trance was interrupted by Sister Patricia's stern gaze. She rose abruptly from behind her desk. 'Paul, how many times have I told you to pay attention and not to keep looking out of the window?'

I responded quickly to her question and turned towards her saying, 'I am sorry Sister – I won't do it again!'

'Come immediately to the front of the class,' she said, her eyes boring into me.

I knew instinctively that I was in for trouble for my ill-conceived misdemeanour. The rest of the class looked on meekly. I slowly walked towards the wooden platform at the front of the classroom. Looking up, Sister Patricia's black habit seemed more threatening than usual and she focused her sombre gaze on me.

'Step up on to the platform,' she said, with animosity in her voice.

I climbed up and stood to the side of her desk.

'Place your left hand straight out in front of you!' she demanded.

I timidly complied. Sister Patricia picked up a rectangular wooden stick about the size of a standard 12 inch ruler from inside her desk and inflicted three hard whacks of the rigid stick over the palm of my left hand. My hand stung with the pain of each stroke and I was left with three red imprints from the blows. As I tried to hide the tears swelling up in my eyes, my main concern was coping with the damage to my sense of pride.

'Go back to your seat, Paul,' she said, raising her eyes upwards and looking directly at the rest of the class. 'Remember children, pay attention to your work and listen to what I tell you!'

I walked slowly back to my desk, my head bent down, I stared towards the floor. Seated, I quickly focused on the task in hand. My main objective was hiding my physical pain from my class mates. The real damage was the sense of isolation and rejection I felt inside. I remember that day as if it were yesterday – I was only six years old, for God's sake!

Another form of punishment inflicted on pupils was wearing a paper dunce cap. Students were summoned to the front of the classroom and stood facing the wall. They were then ordered to place a conical shaped white paper hat with the capital letter D on their head. Often pupils had to remain standing in that position for the entire class session, while listening to the teacher publicly chastising them.

Although I never experienced this form of punishment, watching other humiliated children endure this chastisement had a very negative psychological influence on their self-esteem. In my case the legacy from this pedagogy contributed to a lack of self-confidence. It affected my ability to connect socially with others, particularly in group activities and left me with a fear of those in authority. It affected my speech, to the extent that Mum and Dad enrolled me in elocution lessons to improve both my diction and confidence. Fortuitously, early childhood elocution lessons provided me with a lifetime affinity for the written word and spoken language, which I retain to this day.

For the first few months Dad usually took me to school. As I became more confident, I began to make my own way, either walking, or catching the bus. The distance from home to school was less than two miles and in those days there was little concern about personal security.

My first year at school ended just prior to my sixth birthday. As we entered the New Year, 1952 was the beginning of experiencing a much wider social network, both at school and at home. School provided the opportunity to meet and befriend children with mutual interests, although for the most part they excluded friendships with girls.

Social norms of the time dictated that generally school children were precluded from visiting their classmates at each other's homes. The exception was by special invitation, to events like birthday parties, which I really enjoyed attending during my time at the convent school. Most people we knew didn't have telephones at home, so to contact people from school at their homes was only possible by making a visit to their house.

At home, mainly at weekends, Mum and Dad often received friends; either for the afternoon, or those who lived afar, would stay for the weekend. The majority of Mum and Dad's friends were childless and for the most part, our social network was restricted to married couples or single adults. Those who did have young children were always a welcome surprise. This resulted in Monica and me engaging with a wide range of people. Many of the adults were real characters and had a strong influence on both of us. When we did meet families with young children, it provided a welcome opportunity to build relationships with children of our own age group. In those days, for many families financial circumstances excluded providing children with continuous entertainment. The modern concept of parents taking their children to activities did not exist.

Most adults who regularly came to our home were always addressed by us as either 'Uncle' or 'Auntie.' At the time, this honorary title seemed natural to us, as we were not aware or concerned that none of these friends were blood relatives. The only exception was Dad's cousin who lived in Eastbourne. His name was Uncle Geoff and he often visited us while we lived in Exeter.

During one of his visits he taught me to construct a model aircraft. He took me to a toyshop in the city and purchased a model Spitfire plane. I was spellbound. The aircraft were constructed from thin sheets of balsa wood and the fuselage and wings required covering in thin tissue paper. To strengthen the aircraft frame, an application of clear varnish to the tissue paper was required before painting.

After assembly was completed, Uncle Geoff and I set about painting the aircraft in camouflage colours of dark green and brown. The underside was painted duck-egg blue. To enable propulsion of the plane, an elastic rubber band was attached inside the length of the fuselage and attached to the single propeller. By winding the propeller, the elastic increased in tension, providing the Spitfire with power. The aeroplane took us over three days to build. The finishing touch was the application of transfers in red, white and blue Royal Air Force markings.

I was eager to get the Spitfire airborne and a few days after the aircraft had been completed, the opportunity arrived. Often, at weekends Mum and Dad would prepare a picnic and the four of us would drive into the countryside for a day out. This weekend we all went with Uncle Geoff to Woodbury Common.

Located in Southeast Devon, much of the common is planted in conifer. In summertime the acres of surrounding heath are covered in heather and gorse. Within the common is an ancient Iron Age fort named Woodbury Castle. It is reputed to be England's largest unbroken area of heath land and is used by walkers, cyclists and those seeking the quiet enjoyment of the countryside.[5]

As soon as we arrived on the heath, Dad unpacked the car. He set up three deck chairs for the adults and placed a green blue and red tartan rug for Monica and me to sit on. Although I couldn't wait to try flying the aircraft, we all began a short walk along one of the many pathways criss-crossing the common. The landscape was alive with the sounds of birdsong and clothed with a vivid palette of yellow gorse, interspersed with pink, white and purple heather.

When we returned, I pestered Dad to go and fetch the Spitfire from the boot of the car. Uncle Geoff initiated the maiden flight and the Spitfire soared into the lunchtime

---

[5] Wikipedia contributors, "Woodbury Common, Devon," *Wikipedia, The Free Encyclopedia,*
http://en.wikipedia.org/w/index.php?title=Woodbury_Common,_Devon&oldid=569217333 (accessed December 17, 2013).

breeze. We all watched the plane drop quickly, landing awkwardly on a cushion of bright purple heather. I quickly ran towards the aeroplane. I picked up the Spitfire and entered a flat area of open rough grass.

It was now my turn to emulate Uncle Geoff's flying ability. My right index finger was firmly pressed against the propeller, having completed winding it to maximum tension. Simultaneously, I released the aircraft from my left hand, while letting go of the propeller with my right. Not having the necessary skill, the aeroplane took flight ineptly, landing a few seconds later directly into the lower branches of a large tall pine tree.

The assembled company stared apprehensively upwards into the branches of the tree. The Spitfire was visible, its wings detached and the fuselage severely ruptured. Dad and Uncle Geoff confirmed any chance of retrieving the aeroplane was unlikely. The only way to access the Spitfire was to climb the tree. The challenge was beyond our resources. Mum and Dad quickly suggested I build another aircraft, the next time Uncle Geoff came to stay. I remember Uncle Geoff with great affection as he always listened to what I said and showed interest in my boyish pursuits.

A few days later Uncle Geoff returned home to Sussex. I never did build another aeroplane with Uncle Geoff, but I constructed many similar aircraft throughout my childhood. Life's routine continued for me, focusing in the main on attending school and finding time to play with friends at home.

When I look back on that period in my life, my relationship with Monica failed to get closer. The difference in our ages was only twenty-six months, yet we seemed to continue our childhood in isolation. We only spoke to each other when necessary and there was no sense of friendship, or personal affinity. Having no mutual friends, we did not play together but lived in a vacuum of singular isolation. Regrettably, I have no recollection of any specific intervention by Mum, or Dad into what was a disagreeable situation. We all just accepted it.

During those early childhood years one thing I do remember clearly were the constant remarks, both from strangers whom we met with Mum or Dad and closer friends. Many of these people kept emphasising how similar Monica and I looked physically to each other, as well as how much we resembled Mum and Dad.

However, when I looked at Mum and Dad, as well as Monica, I didn't observe the physical likeness identified by those well-wishers. The emphasis on physical likeness may have been prompted by Mum and Dad; to reinforce the idea of *belonging* to a family, to cement in Monica and me a sense of identity. I am sure their intention was sincere, but the result was totally unproductive. All it really required were lots of hugs and a simple explanation; both failed to materialise.

Mum and Dad were from a generation that were in denial of when emotions needed to be expressed and shared openly. The order of the day, from their conservative perspective, was the application of the stiff upper lip approach and the suppression of inner personal concerns and needs. Intellectually, they both had the ability to think through the issues; yet they both lacked the emotional skills to express their feelings towards us.

For all individuals, identity construction is paramount towards finding their place within society and ethnicities shape an individual's sense of *who* they are. For many adopted people the process is complex, "because they have different parents of birth and rearing and because the knowledge of their biological heritage may be incomplete".[6] Likewise, "for adopted persons, identity development... involves constructing a narrative that somehow includes, explains, accounts for, or justifies their adoptive status".[7] Within many Western societies, "blood relations" form the basis of kinship ties.[8] For an adoptee, this raises difficult questions, "since their familial ties are grounded in social relations rather than biology".[9] For Monica and me, adoption proved to be a key element in our identity construction. When combined with our inability as siblings to build a meaningful social relationship, the outcome would prove difficult to navigate successfully as we grew older.

One person, who profoundly influenced me at the time, was a neighbour who resided a few doors away. I called him *Uncle* Eric and he worked as a police constable in Exeter. He, his wife, and their daughter Sue struck up a friendship with our family that continued throughout their lives. He had a particular interest in exploring the outdoors and spent many years orienteering and hill-walking within Dartmoor National Park.

His interests also extended to amateur photography and Dad asked him to take a series of portrait photographs of Monica and me. I still possess one of the black and white photographs. Monica and I are sitting on two cushions, smiling and looking directly at the photographer. Like many pictures, the image fails to depict reality and is a construct of the photographer. It remains, the only photograph I have where we both look relaxed and happy.

---

[6] Harold D. Grotevant, Nora Dunbar, Julie K. Kohler and Amy M. Lash Esau. "Adoptive Identity: How Contexts within and Beyond the Family Shape Developmental Pathways." *Family Relations* 49, no. 4 (2000): p. 379.

[7] ibid, pp. 10-11.

[8] Harold D. Grotevant, Nora Dunbar, Julie K. Kohler and Amy M. Lash Esau. "Adoptive Identity: How Contexts within and Beyond the Family Shape Developmental Pathways." *Family Relations* 49, no. 4 (2000): p. 381.

[9] ibid, p. 381.

Over the summer of 1952, we enjoyed travelling on daytrips to the countryside. When the weather was good, we enjoyed a day at the seaside. Our favourite port of call was Exmouth, a small seaside town on the south coast of Devon. It was only a short drive away and we had been there many times before.

During the 1950's, holiday resorts like Exmouth were considered quintessentially English. Situated at the mouth of the river Exe, it is a favourite place for sailors. Ferries cross the river to and from Starcross on the other side of the wide estuary. Exmouth is well known for sandy beaches; bucket and spades, as well as enjoying frequent ice creams, were the order of the day.

The town's narrow streets were full of brightly coloured shops, most catering for the tourist trade. Outside their frontages hung merchandise in a kaleidoscope of colours: beach balls, towels, water wings, buckets and spades. Close to the centre, running along the coast, a promenade walk wound its way adjacent to the main road. Except for day-trippers like us, most visitors stayed in guesthouses, many facing the ink blue sea. Many were three or four storeys high, painted white or cream. Built in long terraces, the ridge line along their pitched slate roofs were only broken by tall red brick chimneys. Usually we started our visit at the open-air swimming pool. Monica and I relied on rubber swimming rings around our waists; our aquatic skills were not yet proficient. At lunchtime, we left the pool for fish and chips, washed down with orange juice. Although Mum and Dad were keen to enjoy a meal of cod and chips, their preference was for a cup of tea. After our meal, we walked towards the sea, joining other children who were riding donkeys or were walking in pairs along the sandy beachfront.

Raised above the beach, the lengthy esplanade protected the low granite wall from the sea. Steep wooden steps built at intervals along the wall, provided easy access to the beach. Standing below some steps was a Punch and Judy show, housed in a red and white striped tent. The canvas enclosure stood no more than eight feet from the ground, its footprint sufficient to enclose the puppeteer. Four guy-ropes secured by steel stakes anchored the enclosure into the sand.

We asked if we could join the other children waiting to watch the show. All our attention was focused upwards as the tent walls trembled and the puppeteer entered the rear of the tent. The enthusiastic crowd all waited for the small drawn curtains to open up. A 'Bottler', whose key function was to marshal the audience, heightened the pervading mood. Moving around the crowd, he collected money from the spectators. All the children laughed as the Bottler engaged in ribald banter with the characters on the stage, providing music and sound effects, to enhance the entertainment.

When the show was finished, I asked Dad if we could visit the lifeboat station. Only a short walk along the promenade, I always found this building interesting. Inside was a museum and all the equipment necessary for launching the rescue boat. There were numerous photographs and trophies, depicting the dangerous endeavours of the crew. This legacy of lifeboat history recorded their brave exploits to share with crewmembers and visitors.

Built of local stone, the boathouse housed the single lifeboat secured to a movable trailer. Launching the heavy boat required a tractor hitched up to the boat trailer. The lifeboat station was separated from the seashore by the perimeter road, and to launch the boat, the tractor had to cross the road. Then the trailer was towed down a concrete ramp leading into the sea. We never watched an actual launch, but the photographs illustrating the excitement of the vessel meeting the water as it was slip-launched into the sea was awe-inspiring. I shall always remember Exmouth and the simple happy times we enjoyed by the sea.

***

As time passed, I settled into life at school, making a few friends. During our time in Exeter, we only discussed the question of adoption briefly. As Monica and I began to construct our own identities, this lack of attention in addressing our adoption set the tone for our future development.

In Britain, as in many Western countries at the time, social norms dictated public policy towards adoption practices. From the early 20th century until the 1960's, the process of adoption was conducted within a regime of secrecy. I learned later in life that the historical justification for these clandestine and confidential practices stemmed from the belief that they would protect the child from the stigma of illegitimacy.

December 1952 would be our last Christmas living in Exeter. I had just turned seven and Monica would have turned five in February the following year. I am not sure how the conversation started, but all the family were in the living room, clearing up Christmas wrapping paper strewn all over the carpet. On reflection, Dad must have premeditated his thoughts and ideas well before broaching the topic with us.

As Dad began talking, he explained that many young children were unable to grow up with their *real* mother and father. He implied there were many reasons for this, without being specific as to the causes. The conversation continued with Dad and Mum explaining that we both had parents who were unable to care for us when we were born. I have no recollection of how Monica reacted to the information on her own adoption. What strikes me reflecting back to that Christmas morning, was the information we had received was given in a festive atmosphere and our attention was focused on just enjoying the day. Neither of us children talked about the news we had gained mutually or demonstrated any outward emotion. It was as if the excitement of the day was used as a distraction from what should have been to Monica and me an opportunity to explore the subject further.

I did ask one question. What was my mother's name? They told me her surname was McBride; that was all they really knew. The conversation quickly changed away from the topic of adoption to family relocation. This time Dad had received a promotion to work in South Wales. Mum and Dad explained it would mean immersing ourselves into a very different social culture from what we had experienced in the West Country.

Reflecting back to that day in December, I was more concerned with the implications of a move to Wales, than seeking more information on the adoption question. I just accepted the idea that if my mother was unable to care for me, then there must have been a good reason. This sounds simplistic in hindsight, yet as a young child, I trusted Mum and Dad implicitly. There was no reason to be concerned.

They both explained we would move to a city called Cardiff during the early part of June, the following year. They expounded how different Wales was to England and many people spoke a different language. I would be going to a new school and Monica would be starting her first.

As the next few months went by, I began to think a lot more about the move to Cardiff. Would I be able to see my friends again? What would my new school be like? I asked Mum many questions regarding the relocation. She was for the most part evasive to my concerns.

I realised later in life Mum did not relish the idea of moving from Devon, having enjoyed the environment in

Exeter and what the West Country had to offer. The image of South Wales from her perspective was of a community focused on coal production and shipping. The cities of Cardiff and Swansea, as well as the Rhondda Valley north of Cardiff, had a reputation for bad weather, which when combined with the perception of coal smoke emitted from countless dreary houses, reinforced Mum's view of life in Wales.

On reflection, I doubt whether Mum or Dad had any in-depth concept of Wales or its people. Their view was one based on ethnocentrism, with no cultural understanding or experience of the Welsh people.

Monica and I never talked to each other about the move to Wales, or the question of adoption, until we moved to our new home in Cardiff.

Chapter 3

We arrived in Cardiff in June 1953, in time to celebrate the coronation of Queen Elizabeth. Few people had television; those who did were quickly identified. I remember watching the coronation processions and pageantry decorated with red white and blue bunting; troops of stylish soldiers marching in an array of colours, glittering in the late spring sunshine. Splendid, shiny horses drew carriages transporting men and women. The Queen and Prince Phillip took pride of place, riding in an opulent gold coach through the streets of London towards the coronation venue at Westminster Abbey.

The children that gathered around the TV had never seen such a spectacle. It left us with a feeling of optimism; a combination of pride and a sense of pulling together. Families gathered with their neighbours and watched the spectacle on small black on white television screens. We children sat on the floor to watch. All available seating was taken by adults. Some people stood, discussing the event as they watched.

I recall copious amounts of tea being served, with multitudes of sandwiches, sausage rolls and varieties of cakes, supplied by host and visitors. For the children, there was an ample supply of orange juice and for those who were lucky, glasses of lemonade. When the ceremony concluded, we returned to our own homes. Mum and Dad were tired and that evening we did not have a meal as none of us had an appetite for more food or drink.

During that summer we settled into our new home. The house was similar to the one we had lived in at Exeter. It was semi-detached, built of red brick with a dark roof, covered in sombre Welsh grey slate. We had four spacious bedrooms upstairs. The ground floor had a similar layout to the Exeter house; a lounge at the front and a dining room at the rear. The only difference was a large breakfast room adjoining the kitchen. All the rooms downstairs were connected by a hallway, which led through to the back of the house.

The rear lawn was accessed through French doors, leading onto a small glass covered terrace. Herbaceous borders enclosed the lawn, containing a few mature apple and pear trees. The gardens were twice the size of our previous home and overlooked a large plot of land. Used for allotments, local people rented individual plots to grow flowers and vegetables. Tenants had small sheds housing garden tools. Our property was separated from the vegetable gardens by a low brick wall. I would often engage with allotment holders, especially at weekends, watching them digging their plots and tending their crops. Most were friendly and appreciated talking with a young lad with a West Country dialect, eager to learn more about life in Wales.

Some months prior to moving to Cardiff, Dad appeared withdrawn and unhappy. I didn't understand what was amiss, except Dad's familiar use of terms of endearment, when addressing Monica and I became infrequent. No longer would he refer to me as, Laddie and Monica, as Motty. He seemed disconnected from events and his relationship with both of us and Mum appeared remote. I recall after he returned from work each day, how he withdrew into another room, spending many hours alone. I often found him sitting in a chair in the lounge, silent and staring into space. I now realise he suffered from bipolar disorder. The illness was eventually diagnosed, but remained with him throughout the rest of his life.

For the family Dad's malady created a further sense of social isolation. Mum found it difficult to deal with the grief she experienced from the lack of contact with people created by Dad's illness. She often burst into tears for the slightest reason, quickly suppressing her emotions within a few minutes so as to not hurt Monica and me.

Our response to Mum's emotional containment as children was to suppress our own thoughts and emotions. I recall Monica and I would retreat to the safety of our bedrooms when Dad was depressed. His sullen demeanour made me feel frightened; our bedrooms were a sanctuary where we could get on with our own lives and play alone. Mum would never question our decision to seek refuge in our own private space. Adoption was a family secret we never discussed outside with friends or even between each other. Mum and Dad's containment of their feelings was echoed by our own behaviour, so typical of their social class and conservative upbringing. The solution to life's problems from their perspective was "Keep Calm and Carry On"!

By the end of summer Monica had started at her first school. I had enrolled at St Joseph's primary, a little over a mile away from where we lived. Both of us went to school, usually by bus, although when the weather permitted, we would walk. I made many new friends at school, but found study difficult.

In later years I understood my lower reading level was less than for children with similar cognitive ability, education and age. It was diagnosed as dyslexia but the disorder was not clearly understood at the time. It slowed my progress, making success with arithmetic and spelling difficult. Dad responded to my lack of advancement by attempting to assist my learning. He developed a series of games, focused on spelling and multiplication tables. Unfortunately for both of us, these games only added to my distress. The initiative compounded my anxiety towards learning, which further exasperated Dad's frustration with my slow progress at school.

December 1954 was my ninth birthday. Dad continually pressed me on the importance of education and when I reached eleven, I had to sit an important examination. The Eleven-Plus examinations determined a child's eligibility and admission for public funded secondary education. The options were grammar, secondary modern, or technical school. My progress at school continued to be less successful than my teachers or Mum and Dad would have wished. I tried my best, but progress was hard.

My primary school in Cardiff introduced me to a different culture from what I had experienced in the West Country. Welsh language lessons were compulsory during the school term. I learned about St. David and the historical significance of his life. During the 18th century, the Welsh people selected the 1st of March as the traditional day to celebrate the death of St David who died in 569 AD.[10]

I recall on St David's Day; or in Welsh, Dydd Gwyl Dewi Sant, we had only to attend school in the morning. As part of the festivities, boys wore a small strip of leek inserted into the lapel of their blazer or in their school caps. Girls had a small daffodil pinned to their uniform and many wore traditional costumes to celebrate the national day. The women's costumes reflected Welsh national dress. Traditionally they were based on clothes worn by women living in the countryside at the beginning of the 19th

---

[10] Catholic Encyclopaedia, *St. David*,
http://www.newadvent.org/cathen/04640b.htm. Retrieved 8th January 2014.

century.[11] The costume comprised a tall black hat with a white frill worn around the face, a full length red dress, and a knitted shawl, worn around the shoulders. Below the waist a three quarter length white apron completed the outfit. This traditional expression of Welsh culture originated when Welsh identity was endangered during the industrial revolution.

St David's day made me think much more deeply about questions of identity. A few months before my 10th birthday, we were all asked to bring to school our birth certificates. They were required to validate the age criteria for the Eleven-Plus examination, which in my case would be sat during 1956. When I asked Mum for the document, which I had not seen before, she told me not to lose it as it was an important document confirming a person's identity. As I looked more closely at the text, it confirmed the following information: My name, my sex, date of birth and country of birth. I also noted the certificate was dated March 1955, issued just a few months earlier.

I asked Mum why my birth certificate had only been obtained so recently. She explained when a person is born; a record of the event is retained by the authorities in Somerset House in London. For people who are adopted, an adoption certificate is issued as well. Mum and Dad thought it was better to obtain a shortened version of my birth certificate, because it didn't mention I was adopted.

I then asked my mother if we could obtain a copy of my original full birth certificate. She said this was not possible for legal reasons. This rather abrupt and direct response left me with a feeling of being different to my peers, as I was to find out later at school. Her explanation reinforced the notion that adoption was a secret process.

---

[11] National Museum Wales, *Welsh National Dress,*
http://www.museumwales.ac.uk/cy/273/ Retrieved 8th January 2014

The protocol of the day supported the idea it was preferable not to publicly disclose this fact. Somehow, adoption was a secret and an abnormal process. I realise now they were attempting to construct an easier pathway, both for themselves and me, to navigate the social norms of the times.

A few days later I submitted my birth certificate to my teacher. I quickly realised my certificate was different from the majority that were submitted by other children in the class. The shortened version of an English birth certificate is a much smaller document. In size, it is less than half that of the standard document. As the certificates were given to the teacher, she sorted the forms by size. It became obvious to all the children in the classroom that some of us were *different* and not all of us were *normal*.

When the class ended, many of the children exchanged questions. The natural question was: which type of birth certificate have you submitted? Everyone including me said they had submitted the larger document. When the documents were returned to us a few days later, thankfully they were sealed in identical envelopes addressed to our parents. Children can be very cruel. When they detect difference, those who are not perceived as *normal* are frequently ostracised.

As my sense of identity developed, Mum and Dad continued to treat adoption covertly. This was particularly apparent when the topic of adoption was broached publicly. They never said they had two *adopted* children. Their denial of that fact created a false impression, which only served to achieve social respectability and conform to the perceived social norms of the time. For me it created a sense of guilt and shame to be adopted.

Social changes taking place from the early sixties began to challenge the *status quo* "of secrecy and matching" and as I grew towards adolescence, I began to form my own ideas as to *who* I wanted to be and how I would achieve it.[12] I began to spend more time thinking about where I had come from and what my birth mother was really like. Did she look like me and did she ever think about me? To find out more information to these questions, the avenues of enquiry open to me at the time were limited. Mum and Dad had already told me that all my records were secret. Looking back, this issue would have been the perfect opportunity to share my concerns with Monica, who had similar questions to ask. Sadly I never did.

I remember 1956 as the year I failed my Eleven-Plus examination. When Mum and Dad received the results, they treated the outcome with fear and trepidation. It was as if there was no alternative to attending a Grammar school; we somehow had reached the end of the road. Dad and I had gone for a walk and we were approaching a large rail bridge at the top of the road. As we walked under the archway, an express train roared overhead. I recall clearly Dad saying in a loud voice, 'Paul, I know I keep going on about you failing the Eleven-Plus. It was just so important to succeed. Oh well, I suppose some of us have to be dustmen!'

His statement left me devastated with a sense of total failure. When we returned home, Dad went and sat down alone in the lounge. I remember Mum saying, 'Best leave your Dad alone – go and play outside, and I'll make a cup of tea.' She sensed that Dad had upset me, but did not inquire what the issue was. She probably guessed, though.

Reflecting upon that day, the use of metaphor we use with each other, illustrates the struggle many people experience in coming to terms with rapid social change. Dad's use of *dustmen* when chastising me for failure was in

---

[12] Harold D. Grotevant, Nora Dunbar, Julie K. Kohler and Amy M. Lash Esau. "Adoptive Identity: How Contexts within and Beyond the Family Shape Developmental Pathways." *Family Relations* 49, no. 4 (2000): p. 380.

hindsight probably as much about him as it was about me. The fear of change was endemic.

I recall a popular song of the period by Lonnie Donegan entitled 'Oh, my Old Man's a dustman, he wears a dustman's hat, he wears gorblimey trousers, and lives in a council flat!' It illustrates perfectly how the spirits of the times were changing. Its tone recognised in particular to the younger generation, that everyone was capable of contributing to society, irrespective of his or her social class. To Mum and Dad's conservative nature, the words of the song expressed a celebration of manual labour and access to subsidised social housing - all at odds with my parents' middle class false sense of superiority. They felt threatened by social change and the fear of themselves or their children being exposed to poverty.

The period following World War II was a time of dramatic social change. Britain experienced major changes in immigration policy and large numbers of immigrants arrived from Britain's former colonies. Many people, my parents included, found the shift towards a multicultural society overwhelming and threatening. Both my adopted parents had little experience of overseas travel. Ethnic diversity and a new society moving towards pluralism was one they found difficult to accept. They chose to bury their heads in the sand and refute both change and the winds of globalisation.

In the United Kingdom, as well as in many other countries, rapid advancements in communications began to shape society. The key drivers of change were in telecommunications, cheap air travel, and television. Changes in formal attire worn at work and at home influenced a rapid change towards a more individual approach to life. The increase in disposable income and the newly found wealth of the working and middle class, as well as social mobility, had a profound effect on individuals, making the past redundant.

For many people, the availability of affordable rapid rail and private motor vehicles all added to a sense of individual freedom and ethnic identity. You could be who you wanted to be. You could eat what you wanted; marry, or just live with whom you wanted. You could freely express your political opinions and ideas.

In 1957, British Prime Minister Harold McMillan expressed the spirit of the times on national television, "Most of our people have never had it so good."[13] The American scholar and writer Alvin Toffler expressed the view that the rate of social and technological change left individuals detached from society and the consequences were responsible for a wide range of social problems.[14] Times were certainly changing; it was a social revolution with a velocity of change seldom, if ever experienced before.

Later that afternoon Dad came outside into the garden where I was playing and referred to the Eleven-Plus again.

'Sorry to have gone on to you like that Laddie – I am so worried – I just want to do the best for you! Mum and I will find an answer to the problem, but I am not quite sure yet what it will be.'

'I tried my best Dad, don't look so sad,' I replied. We did not broach the subject again until the end of school term.

Dad went back into the house. I climbed one of the apple trees in the garden. Surveying the grounds from the seclusion of a large fruit tree was a practice I often engaged in when I felt despondent. I had an excellent view of our

---

[13] Harold Macmillan, Speech in Bedford, 20th July 1957, BBC News, 20th July 1974. Retrieved on 27th April 2012 from http://news.bbc.co.uk/onthisday/hi/dates/stories/july/20/newsid_3728000/3728225.stm

[14] Alvin Toffler. *Future Shock*. London: Bodley Head, 1970.

gardens and beyond and the wide perspective helped to change my mood.

***

Later that year, as the autumn leaves shed, our home life substantially changed. Mum's mother, Mabel Hill, who was widowed and lived alone in Nottingham, came to live with us. Monica and I had only met her on two or three occasions and we called her Granny. Mum and Dad told us that Granny Hill would be living at our house and the dining room would now become a bed-sitting room. I found out later she had a problem with alcohol.

A new single bed was purchased and added to the existing furniture in the room. Granny Hill arrived by coach a few days later. I guessed she would have been in her mid-sixties. The day she arrived was cold and she wore a thick, long brown coat and a crimson knitted beret, attached to her hair by a large, shiny pearl hatpin. She wore small round spectacles with frames of tortoise shell. She stooped when she walked and required a walking stick to assist her progress.

When Granny was approaching, we heard the tapping of her walking stick, warning us of her advance. She joined us daily for meals in the breakfast room and after supper she went back to her room, the door always firmly closed. Monica and I grew to like her and when I was not at school, I often joined her for her daily walk.

The walks always went past a group of local shops, one of which was the local off-license. I never went into the off-license myself. Granny left me outside the window of an adjoining stationer's shop that sold children's toys. I would amuse myself by looking at model cars and planes and sometimes she would treat me to a new Dinky toy. Granny went shopping most days. Her deep canvas shopping bag had space for two or three bottles of sweet sherry, discreetly wrapped in separate brown paper bags.

When she returned home, Granny went directly to her room. I found out she hid the bottles in a cupboard next to her bed. I remember the sweet aroma of sherry from her breath. Copious applications of lavender cologne were her attempt to conceal the signs of alcohol on her breath; to us children, it was just the familiar fragrance of Granny Hill. As the months went by, Granny's demeanour continued to deteriorate. The tensions of living together, exacerbated by her alcoholism drove Mum and Dad to find her alternative accommodation.

The solution was the purchase of a mobile home. The following spring Granny Hill moved to a small caravan park close to Cardiff airport. Her new home was parked permanently on a concrete pad, adjacent to twenty similar mobile homes. In the centre of the caravan, opposite the side entrance, was a small double bed, which when not in use, folded up into the wall. At one end of the caravan were two long bunk seats. Each one was fitted to the sides of the walls and covered with dark cherry coloured fabric. Between the bunks was the only table present in the caravan that could also fold up. At the other end was a small kitchenette, with a rear door with fold-up steps, leading onto the ground outside. During the daytime, the numerous windows emitted ample light. At night, small hissing gaslights fitted to the walls provided sufficient illumination with which to read.

I often used to stay over at Granny's caravan, mainly at the weekends. Dad would take me over on Friday evening by car. I would stay until Sunday afternoon, when Monica, and Mum and Dad would come and pick me up. Granny had a small television and as we rarely watched TV at home, watching entertainment from the *BBC* and *ITV* was a novelty. Many of the programmes transmitted in 1957 paved the way for compelling television journalism and family entertainment.

In particular, I recall watching Patrick Moore presenting *The Sky at Night.* This programme on astronomy opened my eyes to the possibilities of exploration and science. It proved to be the longest running documentary with the same presenter, which continued until Moore's death in 2012. On the lighter side, *Six Five Special* was launched in 1957. Many of the older generation, including Mum and Dad, considered it as quite outlandish.

Television journalism was enhanced by two programmes in particular; *Face to Face* and *Panorama.* The former was hosted by John Freeman, a former politician, who embraced a probing and perceptive interview technique, often causing his guest emotional distress on screen. Richard Dimbleby, a significant personality figure within the British broadcasting industry, presented *Panorama.* His program focused on public affairs and became the television flagship for investigative journalism, creating for me a lifelong appetite for inquisitive discourse.

Granny's drinking never caused me a problem. I seldom felt disturbed by her personality change transcending into a mood of bleak melancholy. She was always kind to me, although from late afternoons, she gradually became more incoherent in her speech. She still managed to function – activities would just take longer to accomplish and from her perspective, she had all the time in the world.

On Saturday mornings, the two of us would walk to the local shops to buy food; the ulterior motive from Granny's viewpoint was to call at the local off-licence. Granny would ask me to stand outside the shop, suggesting I looked at books and magazines in the window of the adjacent stationers. I stood patiently waiting for her to purchase her bottles of sherry or port. There were Dinky toys in the window, similar to the die cast cars and trucks she bought for me when she lived with us. Granny was very hospitable to me. Her alcoholism to a boy of nearly twelve was just part of her personality and caused me no harm.

After Granny had left her bed-sitter in our Cardiff house, the room returned to its original use, dining. Dad redecorated the walls with new wallpaper and painted the woodwork a pale shade of yellow. Her furniture, the little that she had, was disposed of. Our six chairs and dining table that had been stored in the garage found their old home again. The scent of Granny continued to linger in our minds, long after she had left us.

Some weeks later, Dad announced we were going to have a new dog. I think she was an unwanted puppy from the RSPCA. Her name was Smokey, due to her unkempt grey and white coat. Both Monica and I fell in love with her. Like all dogs, she only had one master, and that was Dad. Paddy had been my dog, so this time I had to learn to share Smokey with the rest of the family. I often took her for walks on her lead. The best times with Smokey were when the family went out by car and Smokey came with us.

We were very fortunate to be able to live in Cardiff. There were many interesting places to visit, just a short distance from where we lived. In less than an hour by car, were many fantastic medieval castles we often visited. One was Castell Coch, in English the "Red Castle." Rebuilt from 1871, from an original 13th century ruin, it is a perfect example of 19th century Gothic revivalism.[15] It was built by the 3rd Marquis of Bute, a wealthy landowner who made part of his fortune from coal exploration in the Welsh

---

[15] Wikipedia contributors, "Castell Coch," *Wikipedia, The Free Encyclopedia,*
http://en.wikipedia.org/w/index.php?title=Castell_Coch&oldid=590411018 (accessed January 13, 2014).

valleys. Its medieval structure claims a spectacular drawbridge leading upwards to a functioning portcullis and its haunting beauty high up in a beech forest left a lasting impression on me.

Although Smokey had no inclination towards historical stone built edifices, she loved to walk in the grounds. We usually combined these visits with a picnic at lunchtime or afternoon tea, purchased at a café on our way home. Both of us enjoyed many similar occasions, yet Monica and I experienced these outings within a vacuum of social isolation. It was not that we didn't speak to each other. If we asked each other a question, we normally received an answer, but neither of us felt motivated to deepen our relationship. Monica by nature had a pessimistic personality. I was by nature an optimist. The difference in our personalities reinforced our social separation; to the degree that neither of us had the inclination or the skill to change it. The differences just became the status quo. Mum and Dad just accepted this was how things were; they never made a conscious effort to change things.

The first time I experienced in public how isolated Monica and I were from each other, was when we travelled to school by bus. It was a wet and windy day and I wore my navy blue gabardine raincoat. Monica's was grey, both colours matching our individual school uniforms.

We attended different schools and to get to school on time in the city, we both left the house just after eight o'clock. To reach the bus stop, it was only a short walk down our road. We both walked to the stop without talking, which was typical for us. We joined the queue and waited for the bus.

The buses operating on the route were all double-deckers. On each deck, the twin seats were in rows, running across the bus separated by a central aisle that ran down the length of the vehicle. Access to the upper deck required climbing a circular stairway, which was boarded from the open entrance at the rear. I loved sitting on the top deck.

Monica always got off the bus three stops before me. On this occasion, Monica decided to ride on the top deck of the bus, choosing to sit right at the back. My choice of seat was always at the front. I managed to squeeze into the front seat, immediately above the driver. The bus was almost full. The journey would take me just over thirty minutes. Most of the adults travelling were smoking cigarettes. In the damp weather, condensation covered the large windows, making it difficult for passengers to see clearly outside.

Most people didn't speak much while the bus travelled between the stops. Some passengers attempted to read their morning newspaper, continually flicking cigarette ash into semi-circular brass ashtrays fitted to the rear of the seat in front. After a few minutes, I turned and looked towards the back of the bus. I couldn't precisely identify where Monica was seated. I stood up and then saw her clearly; she was sitting in the rear left aisle seat. Our eyes met and I turned quickly and sat down.

Monica was capable of being far more assertive than I am. Within a few seconds, a loud voice from the rear of the bus announced, 'That boy in the front seat isn't my brother. He's adopted!'

My immediate reaction was a sense of shock and isolation. The other passengers immediately refrained from further conversation. The feeling I felt from the glare of the passengers behind me, combined with the silence was overwhelming. I attempted to gaze ahead of me through the window in front of me. A few seconds later the bus stopped. Fortunately, it was the stop for Monica's school. People boarded and disembarked. I looked out of the front window, having wiped away the condensation. Below, walking along the pavement ahead of the bus was Monica, talking with a few friends. She didn't display a care or concern in the world.

The bus continued on its journey. Some people on board started to talk again, others became engrossed again in their newspaper. I began to dread the thought of getting up from my seat. The thought of turning towards the other passengers and walking up the aisle filled me with a sense of deep shame. When the bus eventually reached my stop, I quickly rose from my seat. I felt humiliated as I stepped from the bus and walked onto the pavement.

Looking back, I now understand the trauma Monica and I felt. The isolation we experienced as members of a dysfunctional family frustrated our ability to address the natural questions and concerns we both felt towards adoption. We never discussed the incident on the bus. Both of us felt unable to turn to Mum and Dad to discuss our fears and uncertainties. The event is as lucid in my mind now as it was on that wet and damp morning.

Monica often expressed her anger and sense of isolation and loneliness with cruel and malicious remarks. I failed to respond assertively to her hurtful comments; that only continued to consolidate our isolation from each other. We were unable to recognize that we both suffered the same burden. If only we could have made up and given each other a hug.

***

During September 1957, a new chapter opened up for me. I started a new school in the centre of Cardiff and in a few months, I would be twelve. Dad's solution to the Eleven-Plus question was enrolling me at a private, fee-paying school. From my perspective, it was just a new school; I failed to appreciate the financial sacrifice it entailed for my parents.

Located at the top end of our road was a small railway station. That is perhaps an exaggeration in as much as it was not a grand station; it was just a brief halt. The station comprised just two concrete platforms on either side of the tracks. Most travellers used the station to travel to the main station in Cardiff. For northbound passengers, trains headed for the industrial valleys of South Wales. There were two small waiting rooms on each platform, the twin tracks running between them. The journey to Cardiff took no more than fifteen minutes.

Travelling by train was an adventure. Trains pulled long, connected carriages powered by steam. When I was early for my train, I would walk to the end of the platform to watch the engine driver attending to his tasks. Time permitting; many of the drivers would look out from the footplate shouting out a few words of friendly banter. I enjoyed watching the glow from the flickering orange flames dancing from the firebox as the fireman shovelled coal into the furnace. Often he would join in conversation, his shovel feeding coal through the open door of the greedy furnace. Noise from the escaping steam was exhilarating. The larger engines had cast brass nameplates mounted over the engine's wheel guards. Many engines were named after famous castles and some carried the names of well-known men, or women.

As Dad's office was in the central city, we often travelled together. We would leave the house shortly after eight o'clock and walk up to the station, joining commuters on the platform. Dressed in long grey trousers and maroon blazer with yellow braid edging, my uniform was complete with black shoes, grey cotton shirt and striped tie to match. I also wore a matching maroon cap, sporting the school's insignia. Over my shoulders, I carried a brown leather satchel stuffed with books, pencils, and writing paper.

When going to work, Dad always wore a dark black or grey business suit with white shirt and conservative tie to match. When the weather was suspect, he also wore a grey coloured raincoat, complemented by a matching grey trilby hat. Carrying a light brown pair of gloves in one hand, in the other he carried a large dark brown briefcase, fastened with leather straps. When Dad was feeling anxious, he carried a rolled black umbrella.

Commuter trains to the city were regular. They travelled south from the Rhymney Valley, the last stop being the town of Caerphilly. As the trains drew up alongside the platform, the screech of brakes was followed by the opening of carriage doors, allowing passengers to leave and board the train. As the final doors were slammed shut, the train's guard blew his piercing whistle. The powerful hiss of steam from the engine's pistons began to move the heavy train forward, followed by a large grey and white cloud of smoke billowing from the engine's chimney, and we were on our way.

Usually Dad purchased a copy of the *Daily Telegraph* from a vendor outside the entrance to the station. As the train continued its short journey, I would often peer out of the window and watch a city awakening. Dad would quickly turn the pages of his paper to the daily crossword. The only noise was the repetitive click-clack sound of the train wheels on the tracks, devouring each mile of track.

My school was a few minutes' walk from the station, located in a nearby street, lined with horse chestnut trees. The buildings comprised a cluster of converted Victorian terrace houses facing the street. Each property had two large bay windows, protruding out from the ground to the upper floor. The wooden frames were painted shiny black and fitted with sliding sash windows.

In front of each property was a solid granite wall. Behind it, a small garden lawn enhanced each house, each divided by a grey and white tiled pathway. The path served no purpose, as each front door along the terrace was now blocked off, providing only ornamentation.

Originally, gates had enclosed each property. Now only rusted iron hinges remained, mounted into the stone pillars along the front wall. Access to the school was through a wide driveway at the end of the street. At the rear of the houses was a large asphalt-covered quadrangle, leading to the main entrance of the building. Its function provided an assembly and play area for the pupils. All the rooms within the buildings were now classrooms and the plain timber floors contained old wooden desks and chairs. The original staircases had now been removed and access to the upper floor was up a wide central staircase.

Adjoining the quadrangle was the school's large gymnasium. Secured to the walls were numerous thick climbing ropes and on the floor was a variety of other gymnastic equipment. The school encouraged students to excel in sporting activities. The assumption was that all students were interested, as well as capable of succeeding in these activities.

For school students who were not keen on sport this policy was not popular. Some students, who were unable, unwilling, or just not inclined to embrace sporting activities, were ostracised by the majority of students as well as the teachers. Many of us grew to understand how society treats those who do not fit the norm. I quickly began to learn that to survive in this society, each person needed to acquire the necessary social tools to meet those expectations; I was beginning to feel that I was growing up!

While attending school in Cardiff, playing rugby was mandatory. In Wales, the game is a national obsession. Our school leased playing facilities, less than half an hour's road journey from Cardiff. Every week during the playing season, all the pupils travelled to the grounds by bus. The playing fields were 128 metres above sea level on a high plateau, close to the Wenvoe television transmitter. The site was subject to high westerly winds and heavy rain and on many occasions, the rugby fields were covered in snow.

Playing rugby was not my natural inclination. However, the games we played at Wenvoe gave me a resilience to persevere and achieve to the best of my ability. Irrespective of the weather conditions, play went ahead and I learned to respect the camaraderie and Welsh national pride it inspired.

When I had arrived from Exeter, I spoke with a West Country dialect. While living in Wales, I quickly acquired a strong Welsh accent and felt proud to be Welsh. By the end of 1958, the family would once more be on the move.

It would be expedient if a definitive description of ethnicity were universally acceptable. For most people the accident of birth, attaches a convenient label of kinship to an individual's ethnic group, yet there is a multiplicity of perspectives on what the term "ethnicity" means. Eventually for each of us, personal autonomy prompts the question; which social group do I identify with and align myself.

Each individual seeks to define him or herself as a distinctive autonomous, human being. To satisfy this intrinsic need, individuals need to associate and form groups where their ethnic identity can flourish. These attachments provide a cultural legacy to minimise class barriers and provide a platform from which to defend or obtain advantages both political and economic for disadvantaged sections of society.

The dynamics of ethnicity can be categorised by a range of social phenomena, driven by changes in; demography, race, economics and politics, technology and ideological thought. These dynamics are complicated further by the process of adoption and when those children are subjected to repetitive relocation, coming to terms with adoption is further compromised. Because ethnicity is a dynamic process, it can be constructed, deconstructed, and reconstructed within social groups and individuals. For Monica and me the key question of *who* we were and not *what* we were was the primary question. Our childhood years failed to answer that enquiry.

Living in Wales gave me a strong framework from which to build my own identity. I had joined the scout's movement when I was eleven and eventually progressed from Cubs, to Scouts. Scouting gave me the chance to mix with a wide group of boys from diverse demographics. Weekly meetings and the activities they provided toughened me up. They gave me additional tools to engage with a wider social group.

I used to travel by bus once a week to attend scouting functions. At the end of each session, I would go and buy fish and chips wrapped in newspaper. I used to read any interesting article I could find as I munched my way through my cod and chips on the bus home. Perhaps more than anything else, the solitude I enjoyed on those evenings after Scouts gave me the strength and perseverance to seek further clues concerning my adoption.

In the spring of 1958, we moved to Birmingham. Dad had gained another promotion and Mum was very glad to leave Wales. Granny stayed in her caravan and I never saw her again. I never ascertained Monica's opinion on the move to England's second largest city. My knowledge of Birmingham was scant. The only connection it had with Wales was that the Brecon Beacons mountain range supplied Birmingham with its water supply.

The move once again challenged us all to re-establish our roots in a new environment. My greatest challenge was beginning again at a new school. Fortunately, I was able to establish a new network of friends.

Monica took her pet rabbit with her. Smokey, our dog had died the previous year. We never travelled back to Cardiff and a new chapter in our lives unfolded.

Chapter 4

My first memory of Birmingham was arriving by car at our new home. The road journey from Cardiff took over four hours. Monica and I sat in the rear seat of the car, while Mum and Dad engaged us with a combination of verbal games. Most motor vehicles in those days didn't have a radio, so to pass the time many people enjoyed such amusements when travelling. We seldom played games together as a family, so games reciting rhymes, or trying to guess objects, provided the activity we all enjoyed that competition inspires.

I recall Dad commencing one game by reciting: *Ten green bottles hanging on the wall and if one green bottle should accidentally fall...* and so on. I think we repeated each verse reducing or increasing the quantity of bottles from one to ten, or decreasing them ten to one, over each verse. Another favourite was *I Spy*. The object had to be currently visible; either within the car or along the road we were travelling. It started: *I spy with my little eye, something beginning with...*

I slept most of the way, as did Monica, having left the Cardiff house early in the morning. Our early departure provided sufficient time for the removal truck to be loaded up with all our furniture and personal belongings and travel to the Midlands. The heavy vehicle was scheduled to arrive at Longmore Road by two o'clock in the afternoon and we travelled well ahead of the removal truck.

Dad stopped for lunch in Stratford upon Avon as we were all feeling hungry. After parking the car by the river, our first task before lunch was to check the boot of our car. Stowed inside was Monica's white pet rabbit, which was still twitching and looking no worse for wear.

The rabbit had finished eating the lettuce leaves and carrots Monica had placed in the cage earlier. After Monica had fed and watered the rabbit, we briefly explored the centre of the picturesque town, before walking back to the car alongside the gently flowing river.

We then travelled northwards to complete the remaining few miles and reached our new home in Solihull, a sprawling satellite town south of Birmingham. We were now in the big city and it was apparent we were in a very different environment from where we had come. Outside the car window were rows of urban streets and for all intents and purposes, it was impossible to segregate Solihull from the urban sprawl of Birmingham.

When we reached Longmore Road, we all looked out for the large removal van. We quickly spotted the distinctive royal blue Pickfords vehicle, which had reversed into the driveway of number forty-nine. The driver and two workmen travelling on-board the vehicles were standing outside smoking cigarettes. The truck had made good time - Dad remarked it was only five minutes to two on his wristwatch. After parking our small grey Austin on the kerbside in front of our new house, we all got out and walked towards our new home.

The driver asked Dad if he had access. In response he hastily passed him the front door key. Both Monica and I quickly followed the driver as he placed the key in the door lock. We both moved impatiently inside. Separately Monica and I began exploring each empty room of the house.

The house was similar in layout to our home in Cardiff, albeit smaller. Semi-detached, the house was unlike our houses in Exeter or Cardiff. The roof was covered in red clay tiles and the dark red brick exterior walls were pointed with washed-out cement. Halfway up the brickwork the frontage of the house was screened in white pebbledash. The exterior paintwork was jet black, except for the white window frames.

In front of the house was a small rectangular lawn, separated from the road by a high privet hedge. A large oak tree stood to the right of the driveway. The paved access way led up towards a single garage. Entrance to the rear of the house was via a narrow side passage-way. Dad referred condescendingly to the passage-way as the tradesman's entrance.

The garden at the rear consisted mostly of lawn. A well-worn concrete path led the full length of the garden. Access was via the kitchen backdoor, adjacent to the outside WC and coal bunker. The well-cared-for lawn rolled away from a small concrete terrace, leading from French windows in the dining room. A concrete bird bath on a rectangular stone plinth stood in the centre of the lawn.

The lawn tapered half way down the garden, ending at a large pear tree. Viewing the house from the pear tree, on both sides of the lawn were two rows of single-stemmed apple trees. Growing at an angle of forty-five degrees, this form of planting promotes fruiting spurs to grow along the stem. The spurs were trailed along galvanised wires, strung between upright posts. The length of each array of trees was roughly half the length of the lawn itself.

Our property at the rear was fenced on all fronts with timber lattice panels. Along the edge of the fence line were narrow herbaceous borders in need of new plantings. Mum remarked they needed some tender loving care. Set into the rear fence, a gate led out into a large vacant triangular field. The field contained many trees, including large oaks and limes. The grass had grown long and unruly below the trees and bushes. I couldn't wait to explore and climb the larger oaks.

After the removal team had unloaded all our possessions and left, Mum and Dad were busy for the rest of the day. The Pickfords crew had placed our furniture in each room as Dad had directed. Throughout the house each room contained packing cases marked clearly with their contents. Mum's first task was to find our kettle and sufficient cups and saucers for a welcome pot of tea.

Without much trouble Mum quickly found some packing cases marked *kitchen*. Monica and I helped to open the boxes. Out came our yellow ceramic teapot, cups and saucers, all wrapped in old newspaper. Dad eventually found the kettle which was in another box as were the tea, milk and sugar. Exhausted, we all sat down in scattered chairs to drink our tea, supplemented by dark chocolate digestive biscuits Mum had kept aside for the occasion.

To unpack multiple cartons of china and effects took a few days. Once some order had been restored, the house began to look like home. Downstairs were two living rooms and a small fitted kitchen. A hallway from the front entrance led through to each room below and a narrow stairway led upstairs. All the rooms were fitted with different coloured carpets. The only exception was the kitchen, which had black and white squared linoleum flooring.

Enclosed within the kitchen was a small walk-in pantry. Inside were two solid white marble shelves. High up on the wall was a perforated zinc grill facing outside the house. We had no refrigerator and the air-cooled pantry kept vegetables and fruit fresh. The small marble shelving stored all our other food, including Mum's stock of bottled fruit and preserves.

At the front of the house was the lounge, which was the largest room downstairs. Its wide bay window looked directly out to the front lawn and hedge and the road beyond. It featured a grand brick-faced fireplace. Beside the fireplace was a cabinet with sliding glass doors. Inside was a collection of heirloom silver. Pride of place was an old silver tea set inherited from Mum's uncle. Two small upright oak bookcases stood against the walls and were now filled up with books. The only other furnishings were a three-piece lounge suite and a polished gate-leg table set into the bay.

The dining room at the back of the house had our dining table and four chairs positioned to gain maximum advantage of the garden. The wide French windows provided a panoramic view. Our old oak sideboard was placed against the back wall facing towards the window. A lonely octagonal mirror hung from a chain over the tiled fireplace and standing on the hearth was our old brass coal scuttle with matching tongs and shovel.

In the hallway below the stairway, a polished antique dresser stood against the wall. The back panel displayed a centred rectangular mirror and a barometer. To the right was a small coat stand hung with coats, scarves, Dad's umbrella and walking sticks.

Upstairs there were four bedrooms. My room had a sloping pitched roof, supported by a long wooden beam leading across the ceiling. At the front a small dormer looked out from above my bed. From the other window I looked out onto the back garden and the field beyond. The only furniture was a single bed, a small chest of drawers and a compact writing desk with an old Windsor chair.

Monica's bedroom was the smallest. Adjacent to Mum and Dad's bedroom her room looked out onto the rear garden. Inside Monica's room were a small wardrobe and a single bed. A pink bookcase stood against the wall.

Inside Mum and Dad's room was a large double bed with an oak headboard. On each side of the bed were bedside drawers. To match the suite were two wardrobes. The larger was reserved for Dad and the smaller used exclusively by Mum. A dressing table and oval mirror completed the matching suite and stood against the window frame.

The guest room at the front enjoyed a large bay window. It was sparsely furnished containing a small, older double bed, a low dressing table and a full-length framed mirror, which hung from the wall opposite the bed. The only other furniture was a dark oak three-drawer chest. Adjacent to the guestroom was the bathroom and further down the landing was the WC.

Over the next few weeks Mum and Dad completed the finishing touches to turn our new house into our home. Similar to our previous houses, all the living rooms and bedrooms contained a picture rail around the walls. Dad gradually hung the same framed pictures we had brought with us from Cardiff.

It took longer to unpack our multitude of books. Monica and I were despatched to place them into the bookcases around the house. We both knew whose books lived where. Monica and I had helped Mum unpack all our clothing during our first week, but it took longer to really sort it out. Even Monica's rabbit had found a place to live; its cage was placed below the workbench in the garage.

During the cold weather, for heating we relied mainly on a coal fire in the dining room. The English winters were cold and to supplement the coal fire Mum resorted to paraffin stoves in an attempt to boost the temperature.

Whether it was the wick on the paraffin stove standing in the hallway that wasn't correctly maintained I do not know. However, in winter the whole house continually smelt of burnt paraffin mingled with coal smoke. I remember when the weather was particularly chilly Mum wore leather ankle boots lined with sheepskin inside the house all day. Sometimes the house got so cold the residue water from our toothbrushes froze to the edge of the toothbrush holder in the bathroom.

When we arrived in Birmingham, we didn't have a television set. We only possessed our faithful old Murphy radio-set which was reinstalled on a low shelf in the dining room. It stood next to Dad's armchair, which made it convenient for him to access his array of smoking pipes.

To the left of Dad's chair was an identical one reserved for Mum. After a few months Dad arranged to rent a black and white television set. Men arrived with long ladders and fixed an aerial to the roof. The television arrived and was duly installed in a corner, next to the fireplace. Its position gave Dad and Mum direct line of sight from their comfortable chairs. As the room had only two armchairs, Monica and I watched the set from a dining chair. We all soon learned to operate the new TV's infrared remote control device.

By the spring of 1958, I was in my fourteenth year and Monica had just turned twelve. During our first weekend at Longmore Road, the household conversation covered a wide range of topics. Monica and I were keen to know when we would start school. Dad's main topic was the purchase of a new greenhouse, as well as a garden shed.

As the weather improved, we all began to spend more time outside. Two men arrived and erected the new shed and cedar greenhouse. Mum and Dad spent most weekends bringing the garden up to scratch.

I think it was Monica who brought up the subject, suggesting in addition to her pet rabbit, that we have a new dog as well. I was keen to have a new dog and a few weeks later Dad brought home a puppy. The dog was a Golden Labrador and we named her Sheba. She had a thin tapered nose, with shiny dark black eyes and long floppy ears, a long tail and smooth golden hair; we all just absolutely fell in love with her.

***

Monica and I commenced school at the beginning of the spring term. My sister was enrolled at a girl's convent school in Solihull, a short bus ride from where we lived. The school I attended was in south Birmingham and I travelled there by bicycle. The school was a private establishment similar to the school I attended in Cardiff. Situated on a large parcel of land, access to my school was through a short driveway leading off the main road between Birmingham and Warwick. The property had extensive grounds containing fruit orchards, as well as two large playing fields used for playing cricket in the summer and soccer in the winter.

The self-contained classrooms were constructed of pre-fabricated wooden panelling and each building was erected within a large concrete quadrangle. Within the compound was a rectangular brick air raid shelter with a thick concrete roof, now used by boys as a cloakroom providing space to also smoke illicit cigarettes. Pupils accessed the classrooms by trudging by foot from one building to another. The hub of the complex was centralised close to a large detached Victorian house. The house fulfilled two functions; it was the private residence of the headmaster and his wife, and the rooms on the lower floor were reserved as the bursar's office and staffroom.

The front of the well-maintained house faced out onto a large lawn with attractive grounds. The gardens were the exclusive sanctum of the headmaster and his spouse. Protected by a white wooden picket fence, the garden had a well-cared for cedar hedge that obstructed views of the garden from pupils' prying eyes.

The grounds contained a variety of attractive trees, including two or three high cedars. Around the well-maintained lawns, unusual lush plants and shrubs prospered. All were tended by the school's groundsman who also served as gardener. The gardens were only accessible to staff, and pupils and their families by invitation on special occasions. The headmaster was the proprietor of the school, reserving the area as a strictly private domain.

A large white wooden sports pavilion stood on the perimeter of the playing fields. Inside was a small office used by Mr Jackson, the school's groundsman, who amongst his other tasks, acted as a maintenance man for the whole of the property. According to the folklore of the school, Jackson was a retired professional cricket player. Many times he was seen by pupils returning by foot from a shabby public house, close to the school gates. He would often be accompanied by one or two members of teaching staff who looked the worse for wear. They never looked drunk, but their swagger as they entered the school grounds made it clear they had consumed more than one drink. More importantly for the pupils, Jackson was the go-between for staff and pupils passing on the gossip of the day.

The school was a bastion of traditional values. Pupils belonged to one of three school houses; Sunderland, Dixon and Whitchurch, the latter, my school house. Uniforms were also mandatory: a navy blue blazer with long grey trousers and black shoes, grey shirt and a striped blue and red tie to match. A peaked cap, split half in red and blue, was the order of the day and in summertime pupils wore straw boaters, reminiscent of headgear worn by Barber Shop Quartets.

Amateur dramatics played a central role in school activities. During my time at Wellesbourne, three plays were staged: *Macbeth*, *The Merchant of Venice,* and *A Tale of Two Cities.* My favourite of the three was *Macbeth*, in which I played the part of the third witch.

Many of the staff had a strong influence on me, in particular my mathematics teacher, Mr Brittan. Some teachers had served in the armed forces during World War II. School lessons were enriched with stories of adventure experienced in foreign lands, sparking the imagination of impressionable teenage boys. The school syllabus included French and Latin, which gave me a basic grounding in the languages. More importantly, my three years spent at Wellesbourne developed my interest in reading and fostered my aspirations for the future, opening up a wide world of opportunity.

When I started school in Birmingham, I had a strong Welsh accent that separated me from the mainstream. To integrate with the vernacular of my classmates I quickly learned to assimilate my dialect to a Midland brogue. Ironically, I was able to retain the gift to easily mimic regional dialects, an ability I retain to this day. I turned the skill to an advantage, using it to bond with friends at school and the wider community.

Outside school hours the pace of life increased. It seemed there were not enough hours in each day. Dad and Mum spent most of their leisure time in the garden and Monica began to build a network of friends from school. I began to extend my interests to sword and gun collecting. It was possible then to purchase interesting military swords from antique shops for a modest sum. At school, boys would trade war trophies brought back by their fathers or uncles from overseas.

War memorabilia from World War II was often the main currency at school. Collectables ranged from uniforms, military epaulets, combat hats, ceremonial swords and daggers, to various small arms. In today's world some of these exchanges would be considered inappropriate, if not illegal, yet in the spirit of the time they were perceived as innocuous. My own collection, proudly displayed on my bedroom wall, had three hand pistols and a range of oriental daggers and dress swords.

***

During May 1959 we received the sad news – Granny Hill had died. Mum and Dad treated her death as the inevitable result of her alcoholism. No one cried, or at least no one showed it within our household. There was no public expression of sadness or regret. A few days later, Mum and Dad drove to South Wales to attend the funeral.

Since leaving Cardiff, no one in our family had visited Granny Hill. During that year she continued living alone in her caravan on the outskirts of Cardiff. Granny had been sick for two months, before she died in hospital. This was the first time Monica and I had experienced losing some one we loved. Yet somehow her death seemed remote to us and the distance from Birmingham only reinforced the separation. Mum just told us she was old and had died from cirrhosis of the liver due to excessive alcohol consumption. I just remember her fondly as my Granny who was so kind to me; though I don't remember ever shedding a tear.

One day during the summer school holidays I was looking for something to do. It had been raining cats and dogs and I was alone in the house. I decided to browse through a large collection of Mum and Dad's books, kept in the lounge. At this time I was an avid reader and although I belonged to the public library as well as the one at school, I would often select a book at random from the bookcase in the lounge and take it up to my room.

The books for the most part had been well used, but many of the older titles were covered in dust. On this occasion, I stumbled across two or three small books which had previously never attracted my interest. They too looked old and dusty. What grabbed my attention was the faded gold lettering of the title and author on the books' spines. I removed the books carefully from the shelves and began to examine the first two more closely. Inside the hard cover of each volume was copperplate script, handwritten in dark blue ink, fading and difficult to read. The inscriptions read: *Presented to Edward Denny, for Excellence with Merit in English Language, 6th Form, Battersea Grammar School, 1918.*

The other book had a similar inscription. Inside was the name of the recipient, Eric Denny. It was dated 1919. Who were these two men with the surname Denny? What was their relationship to Dad? I ran upstairs to my room where I had an atlas of Great Britain. When I searched for maps of London, I noticed Battersea was close to Streatham. That's where Dad grew up as a boy.

I looked again at the dates; 1918 and 1919. Reckoning they were books presented to schoolboys in their mid-teens, they would have been around seventeen when they received their prize. If they were alive in 1959, Edward would be fifty-eight and Eric would be fifty-seven. To place these events in context, Dad would be fifty in December of the same year. Staring me in the face was the only obvious conclusion; they were most likely brothers. Why hadn't Dad or Mum ever mentioned Dad had brothers? It seemed so peculiar and strange. I quickly placed the books back onto the shelves and waited for Dad and Mum to return home.

Mum and Dad had been out food shopping and later that morning they returned with string bags, loaded with grocery supplies. When I heard the car come in to the front driveway, I went outside to help them carry the groceries into the kitchen. 'How's the new car Dad?' I asked as he turned off the engine.

'It's still running in Paul. I'm really pleased with it, though!'

A few days before, Dad had changed his grey Austin A40 for a brand new Austin Cambridge. The new car was much larger, but from my standpoint it still lacked the ambiance of the Wolseley he drove in Sutton Bonington.

As they both got out of the car I asked, 'When will you take us all for a drive?'

'We'll go out later this afternoon,' he replied.

Dad locked the car and Mum and I helped carry the groceries inside the house. After helping unpack the food, Mum and Dad put everything away. I went into the back garden and Mum followed me onto the lawn. The sky was clear and blue and the sun was high in the sky. It was turning out to be a beautiful summer day.

Casually I asked Mum, 'Did you buy any chocolate biscuits today?' Before responding, she looked away towards some of the more attractive flowers coming into bloom.

'No – We still have some left in the biscuit tin, Paul. Dad's put the kettle on for a cup of tea. You can have one then.'

'I'll fetch the biscuits and help Dad bring out the tray!'

'Thanks Paul,' she said, turning to sit down on one of the four striped deckchairs lazing on the lawn. As she sat down, I strolled back towards the kitchen. Dad was busy making a pot of tea. I retrieved the biscuit tin from the pantry and asked, 'Dad – Can I help?'

'Take the tray outside for me, please. Don't forget the milk! Once the kettle's boiled I'll bring the teapot outside.'

I picked up the heavy tray and went out into the garden. Placing the tray on the garden table, I sat down beside

Mum. 'Dad's bringing the tea out in a minute,' I said. When I was seated, our Labrador, Sheba sprawled out lazily in front of the deckchairs.

Dad arrived, placing the teapot in the centre of the table. Sitting down next to Mum he drew his tobacco pouch from his sports coat pocket and slowly filled his pipe.

Mum got up and began pouring the milk and tea. She opened the tin and placed a digestive on the side of each saucer. As she handed out our drinks, Sheba abruptly stood up, placing her head in Dad's lap, looking pensively up towards his face.

'Be careful Sheba!' Dad said, nearly spilling his hot tea. Placing his cup and saucer carefully back onto the table, he leaned forward and picked out a biscuit from inside the tin. Breaking it into two, he fed the first portion to the dog. No sooner had Sheba devoured it, she pretended she had never been fed at all. Immediately she turned and looking up towards Dad, re-established her intense gaze. Sheba was rewarded with the remaining piece and lay down knowing from experience Dad's generosity was unlikely to be repeated. We all sat back lazily in our chairs enjoying the warmth from the midday sun.

I was not sure how I was going to approach the topic of my recent discovery in the bookcase. A few minutes had passed, and I turned towards Dad saying, 'When you and Mum were out shopping, I went into the lounge and looked through some of the old books in the bookcase. I found three old books which had handwritten inscriptions inside.' Building up courage I just blurted it out.

'Dad, who are Eric and Edward Denny?'

As soon as I had finished asking the question, I regretted my abrupt approach. Dad didn't reply immediately, choosing his words carefully. Mum said nothing, but judging from her expression, she looked as if she knew something about it.

'I should have told you earlier Paul,' he said. 'How very silly and stupid of me, for not mentioning it before.'

My question must have come as a bolt out of the blue. It was obvious that he had completely forgotten the books in the lounge and the handwritten citations inside the covers. He then began to explain in more detail.

'Yes, I had two brothers who were older than I was. We didn't get on very well when we were young, and after I left school and started work, we drifted apart. We have not contacted each other since. Mum has never met them either. Perhaps this is an opportunity for me to attempt to re-establish contact with both of them again. I will write to them and let you and Monica know if I get a favourable response. It's been many, many years since I heard from either of them.'

I accepted his direct response and didn't pursue the matter further. Dad was not a person who responded well to interrogation.

Mum listened carefully to Dad's explanation, but made no comment to his disclosure of his clandestine past. For my part, I just said it would be fantastic to meet my uncles. I accepted his honest and forthright answer. It made me think again about my adoption and whether I had any other family. The biggest question that kept swirling around my mind was whether my birth mother was still alive.

A few weeks later Dad brought up the topic of his brothers again. Sundays were always the setting for a family discourse, this one was no exception. Dad as usual sat at the head of the table with Mum sitting opposite. He began to carve the Sunday roast with a large steel carver, serving up portions of meat onto each person's plate. Today the meal was roast beef, with two green vegetables and boiled potatoes. Mum as usual prepared delicious rich gravy from the juices of the meat. Once our plates were filled, we all began to enjoy our meal. After a few minutes Dad began to speak.

'I had two letters this week from my brothers,' Dad remarked, somewhat impassively. His tone sounded as if he was just talking about the weather. I guess he found it difficult to talk about his family after so many years apart.

Dad immediately had our full attention. He continued. 'One's from Eric, who lives in Bewdley. It's less than an hour's drive from here. My older brother Edward lives in London. Both are married and have children.'

Monica asked the first question. 'Dad, when can we meet them? How old are the children?'

Dad looked towards Monica. 'I don't know how old their children are. I would imagine they are older than you two. We will all find out more in due course.' He then began to tell us a little more about how he had lost touch with both brothers all those years ago.

'I was born in 1909 and my elder brother was eight. Eric, my younger brother, was seven. We never really knew each other as young children. When World War I started in 1914, my two brothers were entering their teenage years. Our father was a Master Saddler and he died two years after I was born, so I never knew him at all. He died in the late spring of 1911. He suffered insanity for two years prior to his death. He died in a London mental asylum.'

He paused briefly and then continued. 'My mother had the difficult task of bringing up all her three boys without the support of her husband. Life at home was financially and emotionally difficult. When Eric and Edward left home to find work, I was around nine years old. From then we had very little contact with each other. After our mother died, I never saw either of them again. I should have mentioned it to you before. Although Mum knew, we both thought there was no advantage in bringing up the subject.

We both believed we were unlikely to ever make contact with them again.'

Monica and I slowly digested the content of Dad's explanation and I reiterated Monica's question again, asking, 'When can we meet them?'

Dad then told us that in both letters, his brothers had given their home phone numbers. He told us he would contact them by telephone over the next few weeks. He would suggest to them that we either met up with them individually, or invite them to meet us at Longmore Road. By the end of August that year we would all hear a lot more of the two brothers.

***

The high summer months in England are July through to September. This was when we had visitors to stay. Most came for a long weekend and some would stay for a week or more. Monica and I took full advantage of these occasions, enjoying the opportunity to meet a wider group of people. It provided an opportunity to engage with other personalities and share ideas through the spectrum of a wider social lens.

I remember those that stayed were referred to as *Uncles* or *Aunts*. Although we children knew this biological label was not authentic, the expression seemed to us, after so many years, perfectly natural.

One lady I remember in particular was a wartime friend of Dad's. Her name was Phyllis Taylor. When I first met her, she had recently retired from teaching. We children referred to her as Aunt Phyllis.

During one hot weekend in July, Aunt Phyllis stayed the weekend with us. She was a spinster and lived alone in a picturesque thatched cottage an hour's drive away in the

Northamptonshire countryside. Among her many attributes were books she wrote about the Inuit people.

The books were ethnographical, set in The Northwest Territories of Canada. Aunt Phyllis had spent many years living and teaching Inuit children in their habitat, close to the Arctic Circle. Her expeditions to The Northern Territories were conducted over many years. The experience she gained opened up a dynamic new world to us children. Many of the exploits depicted in her books were shared with us during her visits and opened up in our imagination a world of exciting possibilities in foreign lands. That weekend, she suggested I came over and stayed with her for a week.

I arrived at Aunt Phyllis's cottage on a Friday evening in late August 1959. Dad had driven me over, planning to collect me the following Sunday. The cottage was at one end of the village and the narrow lane outside led towards the centre of the small community. Constructed from old honey-coloured limestone, the walls of the cottage were at least eighteen inches thick. The ancient roof had recently been rethatched and wide eaves of bright yellow thatch protected the outside walls. Under the eaves were numerous spiders' webs woven to trap their prey. Above the white front door, sign-written in black script, was the name: *Sunset Cottage.*

The small front entrance led directly from the narrow pavement into a small hallway. The three downstairs rooms had floors paved in stone. At the back was a small kitchen and scullery, with three tiny windows looking out onto the gardens. A small door led from the kitchen to a concrete pathway running parallel to the cottage. A low embankment separated the raised lawn from the pathway. Access up the embankment was via three stone steps built into a rugged wall, edged in rockery stones and planted with brightly coloured perennials.

The other two living rooms faced the lane. The low ceilings downstairs were constructed from ancient beams, stained brown. The larger room was used as a lounge and possessed an imposing Inglenook fireplace. A large high oak beam spanned the hearth. To the left of the fireplace was a stack of dry sawn logs. To the right was a black wrought iron stand, containing fire implements.

The stone floor was partly covered with an aquamarine carpet. Facing the Inglenook was a large comfortable settee and two relaxing rocking chairs, strewn with bright yellow cushions. Below the only window were two bookcases stacked with well-used books. Although the room was well lit, my aunt preferred candles at night.

The other small room downstairs was rarely used. It was furnished formally as a dining room. Inside was a small mahogany drop-leg dining table, with three ornate Chippendale chairs. On the wide windowsill was an old hand-cranked musical box, its polished, dark walnut cabinet embellished with fine strips of rosewood and ebony. Inside, the mechanics of the Swiss device, produced the sound from interchangeable revolving steel cylinders. The hand-cranked coil-spring mechanism provided the energy to rotate the cylinder. When rotated, a set of steel pins imbedded along the surface of the cylinder plucked against a fixed comb of fine-tuned steel teeth. I became enchanted by the melody and enjoyed cranking up the handle of the machine.

Leading upstairs, a small circular stairwell led onto a narrow hallway. Both bedrooms contained two single beds and the whitewashed walls contained Canadian landscape pictures depicting arctic scenes from my aunt's previous travels. The rest of the space was designated as a tiny bathroom.

The garden at the rear was laid out almost entirely in lush green lawn, except for border plants around the edges, some of which were blue Delphiniums and pink Virginia stock. In the centre of the lawn, stood a deep water well, previously used for drinking water, lined inside with undressed Banbury stone. Leaning over the protective wall, clear water could be easily seen below. Constructed above the ground was a pitched roofed mounted on a wooden frame and below it was a circular shaft. A round wooden bucket was secured to a rusted chain and a large steel handle allowed the bucket to be wound up and down the well.

My aunt enjoyed nature, but by inclination was not an active gardener. A local handyman maintained the property. The large grounds contained a rundown wooden garage. It had no doors and was used for storage. My aunt always parked her battered Fiat on the gravel driveway in front, leading down to the lane below.

Aunt Phyllis was by nature an eccentric. From my perspective her vivid personality and individualistic manner was refreshing to a young teenager from a conservative household. During my visit, out of the blue, my aunt posed a question. Had I ever met or engaged with a member of the British aristocracy? Dad and Mum would have shuddered at the proposition. My immediate reply was a very definitive 'No!' In those days social class divisions were such that the idea had never even crossed my mind.

'Not a problem at all!' remarked, Aunt Phyllis. She suggested we drive to Broughton Castle, a moated manor house with fortifications a few miles southwest of Banbury. At the time the property was not open to the public. Fortunately from Aunt Phyllis's perspective this proved of no consequence whatsoever!

The journey from Sunset Cottage took less than half an hour. We travelled the country lanes in my aunt's rusty Fiat 500 with the canvas roof wide open. Aunt Phyllis shared my natural sense of optimism, and for me her charisma was a breath of fresh air in my life. As we sped along the byways towards the castle, the wind blew across the open roof of the car. Her infectious demeanour reinforced my own sense of imagination that believed anything was possible.

Access to the castle was over a stone bridge leading through an impressive two storey stone gatehouse. The driveway swept up towards the frontage of the imposing property. The original part of the fortified manor house was constructed during 1306 and the property has remained within the family since 1447.[16] The castle and formal gardens were surrounded by a wide protective moat. According to my aunt, the castle was besieged by anti-royalist supporters fighting against King Charles I during the Civil War.

My aunt parked her car a few steps from the striking front doors of the house and I remained in the car. After leaving the vehicle, she walked casually towards the entrance and rang the bell. The door opened after a brief delay and a well-dressed man politely asked what my aunt required. She explained boldly to the man-servant that she had her nephew in the car and we both were interested in English history. She then asked whether the occupants of the castle, Lord and Lady Saye and Sele were in residence, and if so, we would both very much like to meet them.

The servant asked my aunt to wait at the door, closed it and went upstairs to make further enquiries. I looked out of the side window of the Fiat, up towards a large window above the entrance way. Peering out was a middle aged male, scrutinising our presence below. His inquisitive demeanour made it obvious he was surprised by two uninvited visitors and wanted to know what we were doing on his private property.

Shortly after the man drew back from the window, the servant reopened the door, asking my aunt if we would like

---

[16] Broughton Castle – Oxfordshire. http://broughtoncastle.com (accessed February 18, 2014).

to enter the house and meet the castle owners. Aunt Phyllis beckoned me to join her and I left the car. We both followed the servant up the steep stairway and entered the great hall.

The hall was spacious and the high ceiling was richly decorated in ornate plasterwork. Around the walls were suits of shining steel armour, recessed into niches around the walls. As we entered the impressive baronial hall, we were greeted warmly by our hosts. They both rose elegantly from dark red velvet covered chairs, clustered around a large stone fireplace. With welcoming smiles they introduced themselves. We were invited to join them for afternoon tea. Aunt Phyllis accepted and afterwards we enjoyed a brief tour of the castle.

We left the estate afterwards, having enjoyed our tea of scones and teacakes and drove back to Sunset Cottage. My aunt didn't speak much as we travelled back, but my mind was swimming with excitement from the encounter at Broughton Castle. We passed through a village where my aunt recalled the ancient church had a particularly inspiring church organ.

'Paul – would you be interested in stopping for a few minutes? The church has a beautiful organ. I'd like you to listen to a sample of a recent organ recital I have been playing? What do you think?'

'Why not,' I said. 'What a great idea.' It seemed like it was the most natural thing to do in the world. My aunt's uninhibited *modus operandi* was really inspiring me.

We entered the unlocked church and walked down the nave. To the side of the chancel was the organ, with an imposing array of metal pipes reaching upwards with two manuals, displaying polished ivory hand keys. Facing the organ was a polished wooden bench seat and below was a wide pedal-board and the organ had numerous stops regulating the flow of pressurised air to the pipes.

My aunt quickly seated herself upright on the bench seat in front of the organ console. She then asked, 'Paul, would you please turn on the power switch below my feet?'

Adjusting her reading glasses, her hands moved to touch the keys and stops. Simultaneously her feet moved across the pedal-board. The church was filled with sounds of grand harmonics echoing throughout the ancient building. Then I noticed a man wearing a white dog collar walking anxiously towards us.

The unscheduled sound of organ music playing in his church had naturally drawn his attention. In those days the solitude of vicarage life next-door was sacrosanct. My aunt caught his eye. As he moved closer, they both smiled politely towards each other. Aunt Phyllis proceeded to play unimpeded, fortunately to the delight of both the priest and her nephew. Any pretext of anxiety by the priest was instantly dispelled by the merit of Aunt Phyllis's repertoire. He accepted her intrusion kind-heartedly without any objection.

We reached Sunset Cottage in time for tea, spending the evening reminiscing on the day's activities. The following afternoon Dad and Mum drove over from Solihull to take me home. Shortly before they arrived, Aunt Phyllis suggested I might be interested in looking more closely at the old well in her garden. We climbed the steps leading to the lawn. Leaning over the protective wall around the well, I peered down at the water below.

My aunt asked, 'Have you been to the bottom of a well before?' To which I replied casually. 'No, why do you ask?'

I turned and looked at the ominous large steel handle attached to one end of the wooden shaft. The shaft itself was still covered with a rusted chain, attached to the large wooden bucket.

Before I had time to think of the consequences, my aunt suggested, 'I could easily wind you down if you would like to have a look. You only have to place your feet in the bucket and hold on to the warp chain, while I lower you down.'

'Good idea,' I replied, being totally oblivious to any potential danger, or potential mishap. Even the rusted chain and the small size of the bucket were no barrier to this new adventure. I was nimble enough to climb in and hold on for dear life.

My aunt held the handle steady. I climbed in to the bucket, holding on tightly to the chain with both hands. Aunt Phyllis turned the handle and lowered me slowly down into the dark depth of the well. The sunlight from above provided me with a circle of obscure daylight. As the bucket descended, my only view was of numerous compact stones built in to the circular wall of the well.

As I descended, I glanced down. Below me, the rippling reflection of still water was coming up towards me. I began to feel the cold from the depth of the well. Looking up, I shouted to Aunt Phyllis, 'Stop turning the handle!'

Heard from the ground, the echo from my voice must have amplified my concern. The reality of my situation must have suddenly struck home to her. I began to feel the relief of the upward pull of the chain, gradually bringing me towards the surface. My aunt's beaming face greeted me as I swung my body from the bucket and climbed across the wall, securing myself again on *terra firma.*

When Mum and Dad arrived and learned of my experience in the depths of the well, they were horrified. 'The chain could have broken, anything could have gone wrong!' Dad said, as he severely reprimanded Aunt Phyllis. She made no comment to his disapproval, other than to suggest we might all enjoy another cup of tea. We left shortly afterwards and although I spent many happy occasions with Aunt Phyllis at Longmore Road, I never was allowed another vacation at Sunset Cottage. She was the one of the most exciting people I had ever met.

Chapter 5

My memories of Sunset Cottage and the long lazy summer days I enjoyed there were soon eclipsed by a sombre English winter. School commenced again in September and I resolved to try much harder working on my education. In December 1959 I would turn fourteen and like all teenagers, I was keen to consolidate further my own identity. New friends and acquaintances outside my immediate family were the main influence in my life. Aunt Phyllis's bohemian influence prompted me to explore my own ideas and aspirations. By nature she was inquisitive, gregarious, and spontaneous - everything that Mum and Dad were not. My parents always welcomed all my contacts who visited, although some friends would not have been their first preference.

A few weeks before Christmas, Dad received a phone call from his brother in London. Uncle Edward was coming to stay with us over the Christmas holidays. Since Dad had renewed contact with his two brothers, they had interchanged letters throughout the year. It had been agreed we would meet up with Uncle Eric and his family in Kidderminster during the spring of the following year.

Uncle Edward arrived by train from London on a wet and grey winter's day. Monica and I were excited at the prospect of meeting Dad's elder brother. His train arrived from Paddington mid-morning and Dad drove alone to pick him up. Before he left, he suggested to Monica and I that we call him uncle (Ted). Dad told us when he was a boy, his family never called him Edward, so we were persuaded to adopt the same moniker.

Shortly after lunch the doorbell rang. As Dad placed his key in the lock, the door slowly opened. We all stepped back from inside the entrance, looking up in anticipation.

'Say hello to Uncle Ted, children!' said Dad as both tall brothers entered the hallway. Ted was carrying a heavy leather suitcase and wearing a dark grey raincoat. He was taller than Dad and wore a grey trilby.

'Paul – Can you help Ted with his luggage?'

'Hello Uncle Ted – It's great to meet you!' I replied. I then grabbed his suitcase handle, smiling broadly and placed it at the foot of the stairs.

'Thanks Paul – you too,' he replied, with a broad smile on his face.

Monica was as excited as I was. She gave Uncle Ted a warm smile and then a big hug.

'You look just like Dad – It's so good to meet you, Uncle.'

Standing back a little he said, 'Monica – I've heard so much about you. You're nearly as tall as your brother!'

Mum was the last to welcome him. 'Hello Ted, so nice to see you after all these years.' Lightly kissing him on the cheek, she asked, 'How was your journey?'

'Only took two hours, Dora, it's wonderful to meet you as well.'

It felt like he had known us all for years. What struck me as we went into the lounge was how tall Uncle Ted was. Dad was over six foot. Uncle Ted must have exceeded Dad's height by at least three or four inches. Both men were similar in build and maintained an upright posture.

The adults sat down and we two children sat on the floor. Mum asked Ted how he liked his tea and left the room to prepare the food and drink. A few minutes later she wheeled in our rickety wooden serving trolley. We hadn't stopped talking, firing questions back and forth.

The room was warm as Dad had earlier that morning laid a cheerful coal fire. As we drank our tea the conversation was driven by a further flood of questions. It seemed strange to me to observe the close physical resemblance between Dad and Uncle Ted. The only first-hand experience I had of witnessing a close genetic likeness within our family had been between Mum and Granny Hill.

Meeting Uncle Ted highlighted for me the dynamics often seen between kith and kin. The two brothers were so similar in appearance. His presence reinforced from my perspective that I was adopted. I noticed that I didn't share the same biological traits and characteristics Dad and Uncle Ted possessed. It somehow made me feel like I didn't belong. Something was missing. I'm sure Monica must have felt the same.

Uncle Ted gave special attention to building an equal relationship between Monica and me. As we got to know him better, we discovered his world view was very different from Mum and Dad's. His world had been shaped serving as a soldier with The Household Cavalry as a Corporal of Horse with the Blues and Royals. He had joined the army after leaving school and told us many exiting stories relating to his military career. He served overseas during World War II and although now retired from the army, he retained a strong physical military presence. His height and stature were enhanced by a well-trimmed, manicured moustache. I recall his black shiny shoes, short grey hair and the aroma of Brylcream pomade.

Every day, Uncle Ted liked to spend an hour walking. This routine gave Monica and me the opportunity to really get to know him. Although we joined him on his walks separately, each occasion provided an opportunity for us both to talk about a range of topics. We explored the differences in our families and religious beliefs, as well as life in general. Unlike Dad and Mum, Uncle Ted took a positive view to what my aspirations were after I left school. I had always dreamed of travelling and Uncle Ted encouraged me to travel when I was older by relating vivid stories of his service time overseas.

Uncle Ted was outward looking and proactive. Dad and Mum's personas were reactive; accept what you're given and make the best of it. Ted's world view was more progressive; create opportunities and then through your own initiative, capitalise on them. Uncle Ted and I both possessed an optimistic nature. Our relationship helped me begin to understand the dynamics between different ethnicities and how in the end, we are all unique and equally important. Monica in particular, albeit by inclination less optimistic, struck up a very warm and close relationship with Uncle Ted. His sanguine outlook provided her with a much needed sense of *joie de vivre*.

Before he left Longmore Road to return to London, Uncle Ted asked Monica and me to stay with him in London for a week. We both eagerly accepted his kind invitation. Our Uncle Ted lived with his wife in a small apartment in St Johns Wood. I left for London by train in March 1960. Monica visited later at the end of April.

My train to Paddington departed from Birmingham New Street station. Dad had taken me to the station and I was excited as I heard the sound of clanging steel from carriage doors as swirling crowds moved briskly along the platforms, either boarding or leaving their trains. I waved goodbye as he drove on towards his office and my adventure to London had begun.

When I arrived, Uncle Ted was standing at the entrance barrier to the platform. As we walked the short distance from the station, I found the noise of London traffic and the swirling mix of ethnic crowds along the streets intoxicating. I was keen to meet my Aunt Vie, as well as their two children who were much older than me with children of their own.

During our week together we visited the Knightsbridge Barracks where the Household Cavalry Mounted Regiment was garrisoned. Uncle Ted had been stationed at the barracks while serving in the regiment. We later watched the changing of the guard at Horse Guards Parade in Whitehall. The Household Cavalry is the Queen's official bodyguard. Ceremonial uniforms cloaked in blue comprise defensive armour with highly polished metal breast and back-plate. The soldiers wear a matching helmet sporting a crimson red plume fastened with a chinstrap. A blue lanyard over the shoulder and a polished Sam Browne leather belt finished the splendid uniform.

We travelled through central London by underground train. It was my first visit to London and we visited a host of interesting sights including Westminster Abbey, The Tower of London, and the famous wax museum Madame Tussauds. The week went quickly and my visit to London left me with a pleasant taste for city life.

On my last day in London, we were all having breakfast together in their small apartment before I was to leave for home. Shortly after we commenced eating, Uncle Ted left the breakfast table and opened a drawer in the sideboard. As bold as brass, he withdrew from the centre drawer a black leather holster.

Sitting back down at the table, he looked at me casually. 'Paul – I've kept this gun since the end of the war. I brought it back from Europe as a memento. I think it would enhance your collection of military swords and guns.' He then passed me the black leather holster containing the heavy weapon.

'Paul, open the holster. The gun's been disarmed and the firing pin has been removed,' he said reassuringly. I placed the holster on the table and eagerly withdrew the gun from its protective cover.

'It's really fantastic Uncle! Where did you get it? Who manufactured it?' I asked, hardly able to control my excitement. It would be a fantastic new addition to my weapons collection.

Uncle Ted looked towards me and said thoughtfully, 'Paul, the gun has been sitting in that drawer since 1945. If I am not mistaken, you were also born that year. Aunt Vie and I thought a young man like you would appreciate it for your arms collection.'

He then continued to answer my questions.

'I obtained the gun in Germany while I was serving in the British Army. Many soldiers brought home trophies of war. It was made in Germany and fired 9mm bullets. The pistol is semi-automatic, the workmanship is superb. The 9mm model was reserved for officers in the German Army.'

I was almost speechless. I turned towards my uncle saying, 'Thanks so much Uncle Ted – I really appreciate you giving it to me. Next time you come and visit us, you'll see it displayed centre stage in my collection.'

I returned home with a sense of regret having had such an exhilarating time in London. I had also met briefly my cousin Jack, Uncle Ted's son. He was on duty at Horse Guards Parade when we visited to watch the changing of the guard. When I showed Dad and Mum the gun Uncle Ted had given me, they were somewhat concerned. After I had told them it wasn't operational, they just saw it as another part of my arms collection. How uncomplicated those days appear from today's perspective.

***

The rest of 1960 seemed to go faster and faster – I was growing up quickly, time was of the essence. We never met Uncle Eric and his family. Shortly after I returned from my trip to London, Dad received news that Eric was seriously ill. He died during September that year.

The summer of the following year was my first serious introduction to the opposite sex. At school the main topic of conversation was predictably either sport or girls. My relationship with the opposite sex was limited to say the least. Going to a boy's school restricted regular contact with girls.

Like most teenage boys I fantasised about girls. Mainly on Saturdays my school friends and I would gather at the local coffee bar to discuss the *talent* as we called the girls. The objective was of course to talk endlessly about each other's ideas and aspirations. Top of the agenda was girls, girls, and girls. Very quickly we all began to make friends with the opposite sex and fantasise how we would make out with a girl. Our chief objective was to have a *real* girlfriend as soon as possible.

My first *girlfriend*, or more correctly my first female friend, was the sister of one of my classmates. Her name was Penny. Throughout the summer of 1961 we met most weekends. During school time we exchanged handwritten letters ferried back and forth through the kind auspices of Penny's brother. Our weekend meetings started at her home and initially for the most part were platonic.

I would cycle to Penny's home where we would both walk to Frestons, our favourite coffee venue. The floor space was divided into semi-circular seating booths, upholstered in shiny sky blue vinyl and the tables were covered in red plastic laminate. Subdued art deco lighting provided a subtle ambiance. The exception was the serving area, lit up by harsh yellow and green florescent lighting.

Reaching to the ceiling all the café walls were decorated with continuous mirror panels. Conversations were mingled with swirling grey tobacco smoke, rotated by noisy wall-mounted fans. Each table had large glass ashtray in the centre, usually full of nub ends which staff continually swapped for clean ones. Cigarettes were cheap and smoking was socially considered macho, adult and glamorous. Most boys smoked to impress and demonstrate their male prowess and I was no exception. Penny also succumbed to the smoking habit as did many of her friends.

Each booth seated up to eight people. The café didn't serve alcohol and our choices of beverage were coffee or soft drinks. For most of us, our funds were limited. Weekends were funded by pocket money from parents or from working at part time jobs. The subject of our conversation inevitably led to where we were going to spend Saturday evening. Our prime objective was to source out where the best parties were being held. In reality the choice was driven by elimination; finding a friend whose parents were preferably away for the weekend.

When we had determined whose house was available, a group of friends would gather to listen and dance to pop music. Young as we all were, most of us succumbed to indulge in drinking large quantities of alcohol. The more ambitious of us would indulge in, or pretend we had engaged in, inept and often clumsy sexual activities.

On Saturdays, when a party venue was unavailable, my girlfriend and I went with friends to a local youth club to dance and listen to music, or enjoy a good film at the local cinema. My favourite genre was horror movies. When we compromised, we chose American drama, in particular *The Hustler,* starring Paul Newman.

Reflecting back, I think Penny would have really preferred *West Side Story* or *Breakfast at Tiffany's*. Cinema seats, in particular the back row, provided an opportunity to hold hands and reach out for a kiss or sometimes a little more. Girls were generally more forward sexually than boys of the same age. Although Penny was a year younger, she was far more experienced than I was. In hindsight I was ill-prepared in the etiquette of lovemaking.

Dad and Mum responded to my interest in girls indirectly. One night, shortly after I had gone to bed, Dad knocked on my bedroom door. I was sitting up reading a novel.

'Thought this might be of interest to you,' he said passing me a new hardback book. I noticed the title on the spine; *He and She*. Without opening the book I asked Dad naively what it was about.

'It's about growing up – boys and girls – that sort of thing,' he said quietly turning towards the door to leave the room. 'Good night Paul, see you tomorrow,' he said, closing the door.

'Good night, Dad.' I replied.

After he had left the room, I placed the book I was reading at the side of the bed. As his steps faded away, I picked up the new book and began to thumb through the pages. The book contained no photographs. However, there were numerous artists' sketches depicting couples having sex in a wide variety of different positions. The pictures were graphic; they left no doubt as to the activity they depicted. They were not pornographic or in any way erotic. At the time the book was considered by many critics as ground breaking. I found, as I continued reading the book, it was not only informative, but was also non-judgmental. What surprised me was the book had no religious overtones. The narrative focused on sex as an activity for both procreation as well as pleasure. Dad never raised the subject concerning my opinion of the book and I never broached the topic with either of them – the established taboo was far too strong.

My introduction to girls was further enhanced by attending ballroom dancing lessons. After our session at Frestons café, Penny and I joined friends at a local dancing school. The school was a short walk away, held in a small dance hall above a group of shops. Once we entered the ballroom the sexes divided on either side of the dance floor.

Penny was a natural dancer. She was elegant and graceful and knew the steps. I was clumsy and awkward. During lessons we were encouraged to change partners. The boys were eager to meet up with as many girls as possible, although the girls were more possessive, preferring to stick with one partner. Penny certainly displayed that attribute, although she tried to not make it obvious.

Weekends never lasted long enough and school soon beckoned. In the summer of 1962 I sat my General Certificate of Education exams. When the results were published two months later, my grades were well below par. In retrospect the failure to gain acceptable grades was entirely my fault. I just failed to apply myself.

Dad and Mum were deeply disappointed. They suggested that after leaving school at the end of term, I enrol at Solihull College of Further Education the following spring. One more year of attending college, they hoped, would finally give me the chance to pass my exams.

When I started college I was seventeen and I was eligible to drive a motorcycle. Shortly after commencing my studies I decided to purchase my first motorbike – or should I say a rather old and dilapidated moped. The bike was produced in Birmingham by Britain's first motorcycle manufacturer. My Excelsior moped was powered by a 98cc two-stroke petrol engine. Instead of diligently focusing on my studies, I was more focused on renovating my new moped. I began the task by disassembling the whole bike, including the engine.

Our next door neighbour was employed by an engineering shop in Birmingham and offered to shot blast the bike's frame and re-spray it for me – *gratis*. When the work was completed I rebuilt the bike making any necessary repairs. The results exceeded my expectations. When the Excelsior was finally ready for the road, I applied red and white plastic learner plates to the front and back of the moped and took to the open road.

My first road journey on the bike was to one of my school friends. He had recently purchased a small BSA motorcycle. The exhilaration of riding my bike with the wind blowing through my hair (safety helmets were not yet mandatory) and the freedom of exploring the open road proved to be compelling. The only problem with my moped, as I quickly came to realise, was that it only had one seat. There was no provision for a pillion passenger. After a few months riding the Excelsior, I sold the moped and advanced to a motorcycle. The idea being a pillion seat would provide transport for my girlfriend.

Penny's parents were not impressed with my passion for motorcycles. In fact their abhorrence for motorcycles resulted in strict instructions to Penny. Under no circumstances was she to ride on my bike or any similar machine. In the end, this resulted in Penny and I slowly drifting apart. As 1963 progressed I met a new girlfriend which was probably not a bad thing. All of us were growing up quickly and needed to spread our wings. Not surprisingly, the year at college didn't work out as well as I had hoped. I only passed some of my exams.

***

During the summer holidays I met a beautiful girl. Her name was Stéphanie and her parents came from France. She was tall and had long black silky hair. Her olive textured skin conjured up a compelling taste for the exotic. Stéphanie dressed casual, often wearing light blue jeans with muslin tops to match. Her bohemian style was complimented by carefully chosen pieces of flamboyant silver jewellery. She enjoyed French music, much of it unintelligible to me. Her long slender fingers were enhanced by carefully manicured nails, painted bright red.

She was both intelligent and attractive and rolled her own cigarettes from dark French tobacco. Her expensive perfume was a blend of sandalwood and jasmine. Stéphanie stood out from the crowd – she was very different to me. That was perhaps why we found each other so attractive. It was my first flirtatious relationship; I was young and immature and lacking in experience. Although we dated for only a short while, to an impressionable young man that period was compelling.

Our conversations introduced me to a wide canvas of new ideas. Her liberal temperament and inquisitive nature were in complete contrast to my own traditions. Stéphanie acquainted me with a completely different cuisine. Her parents drank wine at home with their evening meal, an experience unheard of at my home. The French culture she personified planted a seed in my mind. One day I wanted to travel to France. Three years later that ambition would be realised.

One hot weekend in August the weather was typically humid. Stéphanie's parents were away from home. She suggested I came over to her house on Saturday for dinner. Stéphanie was keen to demonstrate her culinary skills. I was more than pleased to oblige.

I arrived by motorcycle and parked the bike in her driveway. The noise from the bike alerted her to my arrival. She had already opened the front door before I reached the porch.

Dressed in light blue Levi jeans, she wore a close fitting white tee-shirt. Around her waist was a black plastic cooking apron. She kissed me lightly on both cheeks in the continental manner. I followed her inside heading towards the kitchen. She just looked incredible!

The small cooking space was already prepared for a culinary surprise. A bottle of French red wine stood opened on the kitchen bench. 'What are you cooking?' I asked peering down at a covered oval casserole dish.

'Coq au vin,' she replied. 'I hope you're hungry – I am.'

'Very,' I said as she placed the glazed dish into the oven.

'It will take around an hour to cook. Paul – pour us both a glass of wine, will you!' she said passing me two large wine glasses.

We left the kitchen and walked into the dining room, carrying our glass of red wine. The table was set for two. Shiny white dinner plates were placed on serving mats and the cutlery glistened on either side. Between the table mats was an unlit red candle placed in a stainless steel holder.

We sat together on the settee. 'Cheers,' I said raising my glass. 'Thanks for asking me to dinner.'

The aroma from the kitchen began to tease our appetites. Both our glasses were now empty and Stéphanie suggested we open another bottle of wine. My usual preference in alcoholic drinks was beer. Although I had occasionally drunk wine, red in particular was new territory for me.

'I'll go and open another bottle and check the coq au vin,' she said getting up from the settee. Still seated, I heard the sound of a squeaking corkscrew as the bottle was opened.

'Can I help, or do anything?' I asked from the comfort of my chair.

'No thanks – I'm fine,' she replied.

Stéphanie came back from the kitchen and placed the opened bottle of wine in the centre of the table. She began to fill her own glass. Turning towards me she said with a suggestive smile.

'Paul – pass me your glass? I can see you're really enjoying the red wine!'

I passed my empty glass to her.

'Thanks a lot, the wine's great!' I said as she sat down beside me.

We raised our glasses and snuggled up together.

'Cheers,' she said clasping my empty hand. 'The meal should be ready around seven.'

The glasses were large and the wine began to go to my head. I hadn't eaten since lunchtime. By the time we sat at the table both of us had consumed more wine than we should. When the food was cooked, I helped bring it to the table.

The coq au vin was delicious. As dinner progressed our frame of mind became more amorous. By the time we had finished our meal, the tone of our banter had changed to light flirting. We both possessed a wild sense of humour and the combination of red Bordeaux and our natural desire for each other led inevitably towards my first sexual encounter. Stéphanie's mother was a teacher and by nature progressive and broad-minded. That influence had shaped her daughter. Her liberal attitude to life extended towards sexuality. The contraceptive pill was now freely available and like many women at the time, she and her daughter were proactive in taking control of their own fertility.

Everyone remembers the first time they made love. The experience felt so special. We both knew we would be safe, alone and undisturbed. Looking back I remember fondly my first intimate relationship with Stéphanie. However, I now know that long lasting relationships require a deeper commitment to each other, built up over time.

***

Having completed my studies and enjoying the long lazy summer of 1963, I now needed to find a job. The bottom line was that to enter a worthwhile profession, I needed qualifications far in excess of what I had obtained. The only realistic option was to look for employment outside the professions, within the commercial sector.

I scanned daily the "situations vacant" pages in the local newspaper. My attempt to find a position that really interested me was unsuccessful. In reality I lacked the skills to evaluate what I really wanted to do in life. Dad wasn't much help either. His view of the world was focused narrowly in one direction; 'Get yourself a steady job in banking or insurance,' was the phrase he constantly kept repeating. My efforts weren't helped by Dad's continual battle with depression. The world in 1963 was changing dramatically and the winds of change, particularly globalisation, would change the employment landscape forever.

On my own initiative I decided to explore the personnel columns of the leading national newspapers. In particular, *The Times* and *The Daily Telegraph* contained a personnel column. Small advertisements were either inserted by those looking for an opportunity, or by employers seeking to fill a position. I decided to place an advertisement in both papers. The script was brief and to the point; *Young man is looking for interesting opportunity either within the UK or overseas….*

The wheels of commerce turn slowly and replies sent by mail shortly began to arrive. I received three or four opportunities. The most compelling was from a tobacco plantation owner in South America. They were interested in employing a young person to train as a tobacco trader. Although I thought the opportunity was worth exploring, Dad thought the offer was risky and not worth pursuing. My sense of adventure was eclipsed by Dad's pessimism – he was so risk averse. In hindsight he was undoubtedly attempting to be protective.

The response I pursued was from a hotelier in Berkshire. The letter offered me the opportunity of training in hotel management, providing my first week's work was acceptable. I wrote back accepting the offer. Within a week I had a starting date.

The hotel was named The Bear, located in the small market town of Hungerford. The hotel's origins reputedly dated back to the 13th century. The town itself is located within The North Wessex Downs and is situated in an area of outstanding beauty. I counted down the days to when I would leave home. My only regret was leaving my girlfriend Stéphanie. I was, however, eager to make a success of the job and the challenges ahead of me. Mum and Dad, unfortunately, did not display much enthusiasm for my vocational choice, but wished me every success with the opportunity.

I travelled early by bus to Hungerford a few weeks later, arriving shortly after twelve o'clock. My essential possessions of clothing and a few books to read were packed in an old leather suitcase.

When I arrived at The Bear, I was greeted briefly by the proprietor. It was lunchtime and the manager and staff were busy. He asked me to report to his office downstairs at two-thirty. I was then given a key and asked to find my room on the second floor.

Once I had settled in my room, I unpacked my case. I was feeling hungry and decided to seek out a local café for lunch. I left my room and proceeded to walk down the wide rambling staircase and back to the entrance lobby. The Bear possessed no modern conveniences like elevators and the bedrooms were all situated along two narrow corridors, all painted cream. Below my feet the creaking timber boards were partly covered in red frayed carpet, needing refurbishment.

I walked out of the main entrance and within a few minutes found the picturesque high street. Along the street I passed a small café with curved bow windows, displaying some vacant seats. Behind the counter were various cut sandwiches displayed on large plates, protected by square wire-formed domes covered in tight white muslin. I ordered a drink and two ham sandwiches and found a seat by the window. The view was full of people walking up and down the street. Most were women shopping alone and the rest of the pedestrians were mainly middle-aged couples browsing.

I returned from lunch fifteen minutes before my appointment. The manager's office was adjacent to the entrance hall. I knocked on the door and a disinterested voice inside said, 'Come in!'

I opened the door. My employer, Mr Whitcombe, was seated behind an old wooden desk.

'Good afternoon Mr Whitcombe,' I replied politely and walked into his office. The manager remained seated, raised his eyes briefly peering over the rims of his glasses.

'Paul, do please take a seat.'

I sat down slowly, facing his desk. 'Thank you, Mr Whitcombe.'

His desk was piled with an accumulation of business papers, sprawled chaotically over the surface. In front of me, along the front edge of the desk was a prominent customised name plate. Made from light stained oak, it was no more than seven inches long. Inscribed in washed-out fonts, inscribed in gold lettering, was the name; *Randall Whitcombe Esq – Proprietor.*

'How was your journey from Birmingham?' he asked.

'I left home early, shortly after breakfast, sir. I travelled by coach from Birmingham to Newbury. Then I caught a local bus to Hungerford.'

As I spoke, he looked down at his desk, casually shuffling pieces of nondescript paper lying in front of him. Then his eyes lifted and met mine.

'Tomorrow morning Paul, you will present yourself promptly in the lounge bar at six thirty. There you will be introduced to other staff members. From there, you will be assigned your tasks for the day.'

Mr Whitcombe then continued to attend to more compelling tasks. He looked across his desk indifferently, selecting a letter at random from his in-tray. Somewhat abruptly he ended the meeting saying, 'Please close the door quietly – I have work to do.' I stood up and left his office.

I now had the whole afternoon to myself. I decided to explore the immediate vicinity surrounding the hotel. The sun was shining high in the sky as I walked around the corner to Bridge Street. I crossed the bridge spanning the Riven Dun and the road opened upwards along the length of the High Street. I passed by the café where I had eaten lunch and crossed the road, deciding to explore along the riverbank. The public footpath leading along the edge of the river looked onto the gleaming unhurried water. There were proud white swans feeding, their stooping slender necks diving eagerly below the water's surface. I spent two hours wandering along the riverbank before turning back towards the Bear Hotel.

That evening, I left The Bear and found a public house in the centre of the town. I ordered a meal, accompanied by two pints of English ale and afterwards returned to the hotel. The next day was going to be a busy day and I was somewhat apprehensive of how it would unfold. Mr Whitcombe's demeanour had been less than encouraging.

Looking up from my bed at the high-pitched ceiling of my room, the steady stream of vehicles from the road below rattled the glass panes in my window frame. I was feeling homesick and began to question where my destiny really belonged. Turning over in my mind were a range of questions. Why had I taken this job? Did I really want to make a career in catering? Was this small country hotel the best place to start that journey? I was beginning to regret my decision to come to Hungerford. Yet I realised as well, only time would show whether I had made the right decision.

The next morning I woke up around five o'clock, it was pitch black outside. I found my way to the staff dining room on the ground floor just before six. The room was an annexe, adjacent to the main kitchens.

Breakfast, lunch and dinner were provided *gratis* for employees. As I entered the dining room, my appetite picked up at the sight and smell of steaming hot food in a long bain-marie ready to be served. I walked up to the serving area and picked up a plastic serving tray stacked on a nearby trolley.

'Hungry?' a female voice asked from behind the counter.

'Very,' I replied, smiling broadly.

'Help yourself,' she said with a grin.

I began to fill my plate with scrambled egg, bacon, sausage, grilled tomatoes and hash browns. Things were looking up – it was going to be a good day!

At the far end of the serving area were a large toasting machine, tea and coffee. I picked up two slices of bread and placed them into the toaster.

'I'm Linda – If you want tea or coffee, just pour your own!'

'Thanks Linda,' I said, filling a white mug with coffee from the percolator. 'I'm Paul and it's my first day at The Bear.'

'Where're you from then?' she said with a cheery smile.

'Solihull – near Birmingham,' I replied, casually picking up my toast and placing it on my tray. I moved to the nearest table and sat down to eat my breakfast.

'Linda, how long have you worked here?'

'Since July,' she replied. 'My last job was in Bristol. My mum lives close by in Newbury.'

There were other people coming into the room and I guessed they would be as hungry as me. I looked at my watch.

'I'd better get on with my breakfast – I don't want to be late for work.'

She glanced back towards me. 'Paul, you'll probably see me at lunchtime.'

I didn't reply, she was now busy, but her warm smile in response indicated I probably would.

The table I selected had three unoccupied chairs. Shortly after I was seated, a young man of similar age joined me at the table.

'Hello,' I said. 'My name's Paul and it's my first day here.'

As he began eating his breakfast, he looked up, holding his knife and fork away from his plate and said. 'Morning, I'm John and I'm running late for work as usual.'

Before leaving the table, he said he had worked at The Bear for more than six months. John said he liked the job, although he found Hungerford too quiet for his liking. He used to live in Sheffield, an industrial town in the north of England and work was difficult to find. The sixties were a time when the traditional industries of northern England were in steep decline. Many young people had no alternative but to seek employment opportunities in the prosperous southeast and often even further afield.

Following breakfast, I found my way to the lounge bar and awaited instructions for the day. The grandfather clock in the entrance lobby struck a resounding half-hour chime, while the lounge bar was filling with staff.

Even at six-thirty, in was still dark outside. Mr Whitcombe entered the room, dressed in a smart charcoal grey suit. His newly pressed white shirt was dressed with a striped regimental tie and his well-worn shining black Oxford shoes were picked out by the orange glow from the lounge bar wall-lights. Placing his spectacles onto his partially bald head, he found a suitable seat from which to address his staff.

There must have been at least twenty individuals in the room. Mr Whitcombe began by introducing me to the other members of his staff. After delivering some information of a general nature to the team, I was introduced to Mrs McMasters who would be my supervisor. The meeting was dismissed and Mr Whitcombe left for the privacy of his office. Mrs McMasters instructed me to follow her to the hotel's kitchen and I duly complied.

The large kitchen was located at the back of the hotel. The floor and walls were tiled in white. Shiny stainless-steel benches were interspersed with well-used cooking equipment. Below the windows were deep steel sinks, some filled with water. All the windows faced south and the glass panes were all etched opaque, providing privacy for staff and guests who enjoyed the spacious gardens adjacent to the redbrick southern wall of the hotel.

Mrs McMasters introduced me to her kitchen team and then explained the jobs I would perform. The morning shift was from six thirty until three, with a thirty minute break for lunch. My work centred on serving breakfast and lunch. This required: taking orders from guests, serving them from the kitchen and then clearing tables and resetting them. The serving of tea and coffee, as well as soft drinks, was also a function waiting staff had to perform.

After a few weeks, I felt competent with my work. As well as the morning shift, I alternated every other week by working the late shift from three to eleven in the evening. My pay was meagre. The only consolation was the small tips received from patrons of the hotel, which supplemented my income. Time off was either during the mornings, or after three in the afternoons, depending on the shift I was working.

I had no car and public transport was limited. There was little to do locally for enjoyment. There were no cinemas in Hungerford and for the most part I spent my free time either reading, or going for long walks in the local countryside. My work colleagues were friendly enough, but most kept to themselves. My only contact with workmates at The Bear was during my work.

At weekends, when I was not on roster to work, I would phone Mum and Dad briefly from a public phone kiosk. Phone calls were expensive and Dad kindly insisted I transfer the charges to their home account. Catching up with news from home and hearing their familiar voices helped reduce my inevitable feelings of homesickness.

As autumn arrived, the patronage at the hotel began to decline. On many nights, the hotel had accommodation vacancies. Even the restaurant was never fully booked for lunch or dinner. Due to the downturn in trade, two or three staff members had left the hotel during the summer and were not replaced.

One morning after the daily six-thirty staff meeting, Mr Whitcombe asked me to report to his office. He told me he and his senior team were leaving the hotel and they would be moving to North Wales. I felt very surprised by his announcement. I had always assumed he was the proprietor of The Bear.

He went on to explain that he was not the owner of the hotel, but merely the manager and had leased the premises. The consequence of his decision was that my position was redundant, with immediate effect. He dealt with my dismissal in a very cold and abrupt manner. I was asked to report to his office the following morning, prior to the staff meeting in the lounge.

The next morning I made myself ready, dressed and packed my case. I decided to skip breakfast and went downstairs to meet with Mr Whitcombe as scheduled. The door was surprisingly ajar. I knocked lightly on the office door and his voice beckoned me to enter the office.

'Good morning,' he said briskly, not making direct eye contact. 'I have prepared your final pay-packet. Please sit down.'

As I sat uncomfortably in the chair, I noticed a familiar, sealed light brown envelope on the edge of his desk. It was a single pay-packet.

Mr Whitcombe looked directly towards me. 'I have enclosed a suitable employment reference with your final pay.'

He then proceeded to briefly thank me for my time at The Bear, passed me the light brown envelope on the desk and wished me well in my next employment. The process was over in less than a minute. I said goodbye and left the hotel feeling utterly rejected.

Outside the hotel, it was still pitch black. The only signs of life were the continuous streams of headlights from heavy traffic roaring up and down the London Road. It was pouring with rain. I decided to cross the main road with the idea of heading eastwards, by hitching a lift from cars travelling towards London.

I had positioned myself at the kerbside, thumbing vehicles as they sped past. Within minutes, I was thoroughly soaked to the skin. After twenty minutes of futile attempts to stop a passing vehicle, the rain eased off to a misty drizzle. In the distance, the yellow eastern sky displayed the first white and gold blush of dawn.

From the west, a sports car came towards me at very high speed. I raised my thumb in anticipation, although I didn't expect the car to stop. To my surprise, the car began to break heavily and the driver pulled abruptly in to the kerbside next to where I was standing.

The vehicle was an immaculate Aston Martin DB5. With his left hand, the driver gestured me to open the nearside passenger door. I clutched the handle eagerly and opened the door. The driver looked at me and asked where I was going.

The noise from the passing traffic was deafening. I raised my voice and smiled hopefully. 'I am trying to get to Birmingham!'

'Jump in quickly,' the driver replied. 'I am going further north – but I can drop you off between Coventry and Birmingham if that helps!'

'That's great,' I said, relieved to have secured a lift.

I slid into the comfort of the luxurious leather passenger seat, having placed my small suitcase in the rear bench seat of the car. The two-door saloon was painted in gleaming Silver Birch. Its large chrome wire wheels were shod with wide racing tyres. Inside, the cabin was trimmed in black polished Connelly leather.

As I closed my door, the Aston Martin rapidly accelerated away from the kerb with a roar from the twin exhausts of the 4-litre engine. As we drove on the driver told me he was in the movie business. He worked as a film producer.

Although he knew how to safely control a powerful vehicle, we travelled well in excess of the speed limit. The six-cylinder engine thrilled me with its capabilities, as he put the car through its paces. I had never experienced travelling in a car with so much power and have never ridden in such a vehicle again. The sensation of speed lifted my spirits and the travel time back home flew past much too quickly. Travelling home in the DB5 helped me put my disappointing experience at The Bear Hotel behind me, and the experience quickly faded to the back of my memory.

Two hours later, I left the comfort of the Aston Martin. Thanking the driver, I waved and said goodbye. I was some miles south of Coventry and my plan was to hitch another ride. My luck was in. A large truck slowed down, stopped, and took me to a bus stop in the city.

I arrived back home at Longmore Road just after lunch. In my haste, I didn't let Mum and Dad know I was returning home. I knew they would be surprised and I was feeling awkward. I knocked on the door. Dad opened it, looking anxious.

'Paul, what are you doing? Are you OK?' he asked, looking perplexed.

'Dad, I was going to phone you, to tell you what had happened.'

Grabbing my suitcase, he beckoned me into the hallway. Mum came out of the kitchen hearing my voice.

'Paul, are you all right?' she said, in a surprised voice. Giving me a hug, we all moved into the dining room. We sat down and I started to tell them of my recent adventure.

Chapter 6

Shortly after returning home, we received some bad news. Uncle Ted had died. He had been sick for some time, dying a few weeks before my eighteenth birthday. Dad went to the funeral in London and Mum, Monica and I stayed at home. I felt very sad regarding Ted's death. Although I had not seen him for some time, I retained many fond memories of the short times we had spent together. Uncle Ted's legacy was the kindness and empathy he extended to Monica and me. Predictably, Monica and I failed to connect over our mutual grief. Mum and Dad did not discuss Ted's passing, other than to remark they were so glad we all had the chance to meet him. That was how it was in our family; stiff upper lip and no discourse on how we really felt deep down inside.

At the time, Monica was still at school. From what I picked up listening to comments around the house, she was performing well with her studies. As the weeks progressed into the New Year, my focus was on two topics. Firstly, what was I going to do with my life in terms of a job? Secondly, I needed my own transport to get myself around.

I had sold my motorcycle prior to taking the job at The Bear Hotel. During the spring of 1964, I purchased my first car, a black 1937 Morris 8. It cost me twelve pounds. The vehicle was fortunately in excellent running order. To help pay for the vehicle and meet the running costs, Dad increased my pocket money. On reflection, his generosity was probably a mistake. His intention was to help me, but it took my focus away from seeking fulltime employment. During that year, I worked in a variety of casual labouring jobs and it took until September to find a permanent position.

One bleak Wednesday morning I was reading the local paper. It wasn't even ten o'clock. My attention was drawn to the 'situations vacant' column. I came across an advertisement for a clerk's position based at Birmingham Airport. The job description was brief and to the point. It gave little detail on the position, but invited a response by telephone.

Working at an airport had never occurred to me. I had always had a fascination with flight and this job, I thought, might well lead to a staircase of opportunity in the aviation industry. I cut out the advertisement from the paper, telephoned the company and asked for the manager. The operator inquired why I was calling and I was immediately put through.

'Peter Kirkby, who's calling?' was the first question he asked.

Speaking confidently, I said, 'Paul Denny – I read your advertisement in the local paper for a clerk at your airport office.'

'Thanks for calling, Paul. Do you live locally?'

After giving him my address, he responded positively. 'I live just a few streets away from your home. Quite a coincidence! If it's OK with you, I could drop in after work today and discuss the position with you in more detail.'

'That would be great,' I replied, trying not to sound too overly enthusiastic. I gave him my name again, my phone number and reconfirmed my street address.

'Paul, I'll see you after work, between five and six then,' he responded.

'Thanks Mr Kirkby – see you after five.'

I replaced the telephone receiver back on its cradle. I just couldn't believe my good luck. I felt elated.

I always believed it was preferable to take an optimistic view of life, rather than to invite the alternative. Dad often referred to the fact some people are luckier than others. By implication, I was one of those fortunate people and he was not. Many years later, Mum explained how Dad resented my sense of eternal optimism and Dad was jealous of my sanguine nature. To be fair, fate often dispensed the cards of fortune out unevenly.

The rest of Wednesday went more slowly than I would have liked. I paced around the house restlessly. Dad was at work, Monica was at school, and Mum was home as usual.

'Are you going out today?' Mum asked, as I walked into the kitchen. She had started preparing lunch. 'I heard you speaking on the phone. I expect you're feeling hungry.'

I tried not to sound too optimistic. 'I'm going out later on Mum. I've got a job interview.'

I briefly explained that my phone call earlier was about a job. It involved working at the airport. Mum seemed pleased, but surprised. 'I hope you get the job. What do they want you to do?'

'I'm not really sure, but I should know more later on.'

'You had better look your best and change into your suit,' she said encouragingly.

'Mum, the interview is after five this evening. They're going to pick me up.'

'How unusual!' she replied.

'The man lives close by, he said he'd call in on his way home from work.'

'Well, good luck – make sure you look your best,' she replied, continuing to peel the lunchtime vegetables.

I had changed into my only suit for the interview, and by five o'clock I sat waiting patiently in the dining room. Mum was reading as I entered the room and Monica was upstairs in her room doing her homework.

'You look very smart Paul, I like your tie,' she said, looking up towards me with an encouraging smile.

'I hope Dad will be pleased,' I said.

'I'm *sure* he will dear,' she replied, rather doubtfully.

I turned on the television. I was feeling a little anxious. Just before six, I heard a car turn into the driveway.

'Mum – That sounds like a car outside, I'll see you later – bye!' I said, on my way out.

'Good luck Paul,' Mum said.

I opened the door and a green Mini was parked in the driveway. The engine was running. Inside, a short, stocky man, wearing glasses, stepped out briskly from behind the wheel. He was dressed in a dark suit sporting a bright red tie.

'Hello, I'm Paul. Thanks for coming over to meet me.'

Shaking my hand firmly, he said, 'Peter Kirkby – glad to meet you. Let's drive over to my place and chat about the job?'

I climbed into the car, sitting back in the hand-stitched, contoured, leather racing seat. The vehicle had been modified and as the engine started, the throb of the exhaust beckoned the engine to perform. Once we were out on the open road, Peter Kirkby looked across and said, 'Paul, I'm sure you have some questions about the opportunity. We'll be at my place in a couple of minutes – and please – call me Peter!'

'Thanks Peter,' I said, encouraged by his laid-back approach.

As we drove on, it was clear the car was capable of high levels of performance. The droning from the straight-through exhaust and the feel of the hard suspension of the Mini Cooper, confirmed the driver as a motoring enthusiast. We established a good connection immediately.

The interview lasted less than an hour. As we drove back to Longmore Road, my new boss offered me the job, which I immediately accepted. We agreed I would start the following Monday at nine o'clock. Working hours were from nine to five, Monday to Friday and I was required to work every other Saturday morning until noon.

Peter dropped me off outside my home. I said goodbye, thanked him again for the opportunity, and let myself into the house. Mum and Dad were sitting quietly in the dining room, having just finished their evening meal.

'How did it go?' Mum asked, as I entered the room.

'Fantastic!' I said. 'I got the job – I start next Monday.'

Dad looked up rather casually from reading his newspaper.

'Mum told me the job's at the airport. Well done,' he remarked, looking over the rim of his bifocals. Somehow, the tone of his remark lacked my sense of enthusiasm.

'Take a seat at the table Paul, I'll fetch your dinner from the oven,' Mum said, leaving the room.

'I'll be able to travel to work in my new car Dad,' I said, hoping he would show a little more enthusiasm.

'Sounds sensible to me,' he said. 'I just hope this job is what you want and it works out well for you.'

That was the end of the conversation. In my head, I could hear Dad's familiar words of subdued resignation when faced with a fait accompli. 'It's your life Paul – we have done our best – we cannot do any more.' After dinner, I decided to go to bed early and immerse myself in a good book.

***

I started my new job at the airport in September 1964. The short journey in my refurbished Morris 8 took less than thirty minutes. I was the youngest member of a team of eight. As the months progressed, I moved between the airport and city offices, learning basic bookkeeping and the intricacies of preparing import-export documentation.

I felt comfortable working at the airport. I enjoyed the work and acquired a wide group of new friends. My progress was rewarded with a pay rise and in the spring of 1965 I decided to buy my first brand new car. I chose a green Morris Mini, which I bought on hire purchase. The car was similar to Peter Kirkby's Mini Cooper, but lacked the sporting refinements.

Now that my mediocre weekly wage had increased, it allowed me to become more self-sufficient. I was still living at home and gave Mum a token contribution towards food and accommodation. Most of my income after I had paid my weekly hire purchase commitment went on entertainment.

Airports have an ambiance of their own and provide a lively social environment – Birmingham was no exception. The main terminal building had excellent facilities for eating and drinking and I took full advantage of the opportunity. The good life it represented attracted numerous ambitious young men and women. Many saw the rapid expansion of the aviation industry as a worthwhile career opportunity. Not least was the compelling attraction of a lifestyle touched with glamour.

Shortly after I started working at the airport, I developed a relationship with one of my work colleagues. Her name was Judy, an identical twin. Her twin sister Janet also worked at the airport with another organisation. We all got on like a house on fire and in the summer of the following year, Judy and I become engaged. We came from very different social backgrounds. Our youthful intoxication and infatuation with each other quickly led towards marriage.

I first met Judy after she had just broken up from a previous relationship. The twin sisters had celebrated their engagements together the previous year. When we got engaged, Janet's relationship was progressing towards marriage the following year. In those days, many young couples were married in their early twenties.

Whether or not it was a combination of expectations, prompted by future in-laws, or the expectations of marriage from our peers, it led us both down the slippery slope towards complying with the social norms of the period. In hindsight, we both needed more time and experience of life to temper our individual needs. We were immature, but the influence of social conventions decided our future fate. Looking back, neither of us was fully prepared for marriage, but then who really is!

Following our engagement, I continued to enjoy a range of leisure activities I had engaged in prior to working at the airport. Before meeting Judy, I had learned to play the drums. My skills were proficient enough to be able to join a local amateur rock band. To practice, I used my bedroom, which was not an ideal venue. Mum and Dad tolerated my newfound passion, but due to the noise, Dad decided to line my bedroom walls and ceiling with polystyrene sheeting. His plan was an attempt to isolate the noise from the rest of the house. The end result was minimal. The combined sound of drums and three guitars played by fellow band mates must have driven the household crazy – as well as our tolerant and considerate neighbours.

My other passion, collecting swords and small arms, eventually shifted to an interest in rough shooting. I was fortunate to have access to farming land through a couple of old school friends. In England, this type of hunting is often performed with dogs, especially trained for the gun. I usually shot with friends. Traditionally, several hunters walk through woodland, fields or moorland and the dogs, put up the birds. After the game is shot, the dogs retrieve them.

My friends and I did not have the advantage of a dog trained for the gun and had to retrieve the catch ourselves. If we were lucky, we would encounter a stray pheasant. For the most part, we were content to shoot rabbit or pigeon. Nowadays in England, most people require a membership of a syndicate, which provides for the rearing of game and the maintenance of the habitat. We were fortunate; we enjoyed our sport through the generosity of local farming families.

During 1965, I became politically active. I joined the *Campaign for Nuclear Disarmament*. This appealed to my liberal inclination and nurtured my growing left-wing sympathies. Back when I was completing my final studies at Solihull College, two friends in particular introduced me to socialism and activist ideas, and meeting like-minded young men and women. This gave me a forum from which to explore a range of idealistic ideas compelling to young adults.

The political discourse we embraced focused on ideas emanating from the political left. We met in less than salubrious public houses, often located in rundown areas of Birmingham's inner city. Most of us drank large quantities of cheap rough cider, bitter or mild beer, all consumed in a thick fog of grey cigarette smoke. The men mostly wore fawn Duffel coats. This stereotype dress code of the student left was made from thick course woollen fabric, lined with a woolly tartan pattern. The coat had a bucket hood and the outfit was fastened at the front by wooden toggles.

Karl Marx and Frederick Engel's were often the topic of conversation. During meetings at the pub, Marx's *Das Capital* came up for discussion. I recall on one occasion a well-thumbed copy was eagerly thrust into my naïve political hands. The intention from my activist friends was I would digest its contents and its critique of the political economy.

I never did read the whole book. Many of the ideas Marx expounded aroused in me a sense of injustice about the capitalist system, where the motivating force is the exploitation of labour and the benefit of unpaid work is ultimately converted into profit and surplus value. My youthful flirtation with idealism eventually swung towards realism. I was soon to become engaged to be married.

***

I had always wanted to visit France. My job at the airport provided me with the opportunity to obtain concessionary priced air tickets. At the time, there were few international flights from Birmingham Airport. British European Airways and Aer Lingus predominantly served the whole market and the former operated a daily flight to and from Paris. I had never flown before and I decided to take one week's vacation in July 1965. Accompanying me on the trip was an old school friend, Robert who joined me at the airport on a wet Sunday morning. We boarded the plane to Paris at around eleven o'clock. The aircraft on the route was a Vickers Viscount. The four engine jet turbo-prop employed a new form of propulsion, replacing the conventional piston engine. I can still feel that initial excitement; for both of us it was our first journey outside the United Kingdom.

After the crew ordered the closure of the doors, the Rolls Royce Dart engines were individually started. We sat back in our narrow seats as the aircraft taxied slowly towards the head of the runway. As we approached the take-off position, the cabin crew read out the safety instructions. Finally, a visual inspection of all passengers was made to check all seatbelts were correctly fastened.

The plane seated seventy-five passengers. I sat in a window seat, while Robert sat next to the aisle. Most of the passengers were dressed formally. Robert and I wore long trousers and sport jackets with white shirts and ties. In those days air travel was a new experience for most people, the occasion warranted dressing up, and looking one's best.

Once the aircraft had climbed to its cruising altitude, the cabin crew served a light lunch of chicken with salad served on blue plastic trays. We were all offered a choice of free beer or wine with our meal, followed by tea or coffee. We naturally could not resist the temptation of ordering a beer and a glass of red wine. As we sat enjoying our lunch, the wide panoramic window gave us both a splendid view of the English Channel below.

Our scheduled flight time was just under ninety minutes. Shortly after we had finished our coffee, the Viscount began its slow descent into Le Bourget. As the aircraft descended, the captain announced we would be arriving a few minutes later than scheduled, due to strong head winds. He thanked all passengers for flying with BEA, hoping we all had enjoyed the flight. Following the captain's announcement, cabin staff instructed us to fasten our seat belts tightly and return our seat backs to the upright position.

The Viscount tyres screeched on touching the runway and the combination of the heavy application of brakes, with the feathering of the propeller blades, rapidly reduced the aircraft's speed. The captain turned the plane off the main runway and we headed towards the terminal building feeling full of excitement about the adventure ahead of us.

Passing through French customs, we collected our small suitcases from the clunking baggage carousel. We entered the main concourse of the terminal and our first impression was the unfamiliar sound of foreign voices. All around us were rushing crowds, entering and leaving the building.

Many people were drinking coffee with an alcohol drink on the side. Some patrons drank, leaning against long zinc counters. Most smoked. The unfamiliar sharp odour from pungent Gallic tobacco cut the air. We quickly recognised the large *sortie* signage indicating the exit and ventured with our shabby cases out of the terminal.

Robert and I had taken French lessons while at school. The result to say the least was less than impressive. We both managed to read most of the signage and advertisements in the terminal building. However, to listen and comprehend rapidly spoken conversation in French was way beyond our expertise. We walked towards the taxi rank and joined the long queue. As we stood and waited, we both began to construct in our minds a suitable phrase in French, advising our driver of our intended destination.

Our central city hotel was pre-booked and situated in a street a few hundred metres from the Arc de Triomphe. Eventually we managed to secure a taxi, a small battered Citroen. Our driver spoke English as badly as we spoke French. Yet we somehow successfully managed to communicate as we travelled towards our hotel. Looking out of the windows both of us were engrossed by the change of landscape compared to dreary England. Along the roadside leading to the central city were numerous large advertising billboards titillating potential consumers with their seductive messages with a Latin twist. Most were advocating hard liquor, beer or cigarettes, while some featured seductive models promoting cosmetics or perfumes. After a while, we both knew we were approaching our destination as in the distance stood the stark structural edifice of the Eiffel tower.

The taxi-driver was friendly and he told us he had originally emigrated from Algeria in the 1950's. Like taxi-drivers the world over, he knew how to converse and as he drove through the dreary suburbs towards the city, he gave us a condensed synopsis of his life in broken English and French. He had married a French girl two years after he arrived in France, they had two young children and lived in an apartment in the outer suburbs. As he began to explain further his aspirations for the future, the cab stopped abruptly at our hotel.

We alighted from the Citroen in the Rue La Boétie, paid our driver, and carried our cases towards the entrance steps of the hotel. Looking up, our initial impression of the exterior was less striking than we had envisaged. The accommodation was what the French call *la pension,* a boarding house accommodation, often managed by one family.

The street entrance led directly in to a *petite* entrance lobby located on the ground floor. A small, dark mahogany reception desk occupied a space next to a narrow undersized elevator. Mounted on the back wall of the desk was a dark wooden rectangular frame with uniquely numbered pigeonhole spaces. Some of the open spaces had room keys attached to white ceramic key holders. Many contained letters, waiting to be claimed by their guests.

The dim lighting in the reception area came from an elegant brass chandelier. It hung precariously from a decorative plaster ceiling rose. Shaded by pear-shaped glass shades, two of them were defective. The chandelier's utility was enhanced by the reflection from two large gilded mirrors mounted on opposing walls.

The desk was unattended when we arrived. A discreet notice on top of the desk in French, English and German invited visitors to ring a brass bell. We must have rung the bell three or four times. Eventually, a middle-aged woman with grey hair, dressed conservatively in a dark blue dress, appeared from a narrow hallway leading out into the reception area. We must have both looked typically English to her as she spoke in broken English asking whether we had made a reservation. I replied, saying our accommodation had been booked for two weeks. After confirming our booking, she asked us to surrender our passports, having explained all guests were subject to a mandatory police check. Once we had signed the visitor's book, she handed us the key. Room twenty-seven was on the fifth floor.

According to the brochure, the pension comprised thirty guest rooms on six levels. On the ground floor was a small breakfast room where *petit déjeuner* was available for guests. Access to the upper floors was via a steep stone stairwell or a small traction elevator. I slid back the steel elevator gate, we placed our cases on the floor space in front of us, and we managed to squeeze ourselves into the confined space that was left. Robert shut the internal protective gate and pressed the brass push button to the fifth floor. Slowly, the creaking lift ascended.

Our room was halfway down a windowless dark corridor with dim sidelights along the wall. Having turned the large key in the lock, I swung upon the door and we entered the room placing our suitcase below each single bed. The window shutters were closed. I turned the centre latch and swung both hinged shutters back against the wall. The bright afternoon sunshine flooded the room.

The bedroom window looked out over a narrow stone balcony, facing towards the street. The parquetry floor, in rich brown mahogany, made the room look much larger than it was. Between the beds was a small table and lying in front was a rectangular Persian carpet. On the opposing wall were two small gilded mirrors. In one corner of the room a modest tiled bathroom fitted with white ceramic porcelain, filled the space. It was only sufficient for a small bath, toilet, bidet and washbasin. The main room featured a high ceiling, decorated with ornate plasterwork, giving the room certain elegance. The space had no other furnishings, save two small bedside lights fitted on the wall.

We left our cases in the room. Robert and I had no inclination to unpack our belongings, as we were eager to explore outside. Leaving the room securely locked, we boarded the creaking lift and descended to the ground floor. The reception area was still unoccupied and we walked out onto the street.

Both of us were thirsty. We headed right towards the Champs-Élysées to find a café to our liking. The distance was less than fifty metres. As we walked towards the intersection, we passed a small licensed tobacconist. After entering the *Tabac,* we purchased two packets of unfiltered Gauloise cigarettes packaged in distinctive light blue soft-top packets. Smoking was a habit we had acquired after leaving school. In France, cigarettes were much cheaper than in England.

Walking down the Avenue des Champs-Élysées, we were both struck by the cultural contrast. Reaching from the Arc de Triomphe in the west, to the Place de la Concorde in the east, the avenues' expensive real estate created an ambiance for fashionable restaurants, luxury speciality shops, and cinema complexes. Along the sidewalk of the famous promenade were tidily clipped horse-chestnut trees. The distinctive smell from Turkish tobacco lingered in the air. A range of busy colourful cafés had tables and chairs spread out towards the roadway. Pedestrians paraded up and down the main thoroughfare. Beautiful, well-dressed women caught our gaze, some strolling with small dogs as elegant as their owners. Waiters nimbly worked their way through the cluster of seated patrons, waiting for service.

The café we chose had an array of aluminium tables on the forecourt outside, surrounded by well-worn rattan chairs. Brightly coloured red and white umbrellas protected the clientele from the elements. Tables were all set with white linen, secured against the light breeze by bright steel clips secured to the tables' edges. In the middle was a large glass ashtray and a classy leather bound menu stood centre stage.

As soon as we were seated, a waiter appeared. It was only four o'clock, but we opted for a beer. Our well-rehearsed request seemed to strike the right note, *'Garçon – deux grosses bières, s'il vous plait?'* Within a few minutes, two large glasses of cold tap beer were on our table.

'Cheers Robert,' I said, as we both lifted our glasses.

'Like-wise! I think we're going to have a great time! Cheers!' said Robert, looking back across the table.

'Let's try one of those Gauloise cigarettes' I said, bringing out my Zippo lighter.

I opened my packet, withdrew one, and lit it up.

'Pass the lighter – I didn't buy any matches.' Robert said.

Tongue in cheek I grinned and said, 'You're always trying to save money – you're getting to sound a bit like me.'

We left the café after a couple of beers. It had turned past five o'clock and we decided to go back to the *pension* and change for dinner. Our last meal was on board the Viscount; we were both ravenous.

It was getting towards dusk, when we finally set out again from our hotel. We took the Metro to Montmartre, getting off at Abbesses, the nearest station. We quickly found a place to eat. Fortunately, all French restaurants are required to publish their menu outside their premises so patrons know what to expect. We were in luck and the waiter took us straight to a table.

If we had been more astute, we would not have eaten at that restaurant. The food and drink were excellent and we over-indulged. We had no credit card, so we paid in cash.

The total for food, drink and service charges, were far greater than we had anticipated. The extra bottle of red Bordeaux plus a few beers, not to mention the cups of *café noir* and cognac, didn't come cheaply. We split the account and left the premises, deciding to walk back to our *Pension* on Rue La Boétie.

The next morning we woke up shortly before dawn to the sound of water flushing down the street below. I went to the window and looked over the balcony. Below in the street were janitors, opening and shutting hydrant valves, discharging clean water along the gutters. Garbage was being swept up and loaded onto trucks. What a brilliant idea; why didn't the English emulate the French and adopt a similar practice?

Having both washed and dressed, Robert and I made ourselves ready for the day ahead. We left our room before eight o'clock, deciding to have *croissants avec du café*, in the hotel breakfast room downstairs. The room was empty when we arrived and we sat at a small table close to the door. A round table across the room was covered in white linen and in the centre was two large brown wicker baskets, containing freshly baked croissants. The aroma was delicious. After helping ourselves, we went back to our table generously applying butter and jam. A young female waitress arrived just after we had started to eat. She smiled and asked us for our room number and what we wanted to drink. We both ordered *café noir.* Having finished our breakfast, we left our keys at the desk and exited on to Rue La Boétie. The street was bustling with pedestrians and thick with fumes from busy traffic.

As we had only a week in Paris, time was of the essence. We had purchased a Paris guide with a concise colour map of the city. Both of us were keen to spend the short time seeing the sights, either travelling by Metro, or preferably walking between the main attractions. Our first point of call was the Eiffel Tower. We ascended by elevator, riding to the first floor. Then we climbed a series of steep steps, which eventually took us up to a ballroom on the top deck of the landmark edifice. The views across Paris were breath-taking.

Our next stop was the Panthéon. Construction began in 1758 and the impressive stone building was completed in 1790 following the beginning of the French Revolution. The neoclassical building, originally conceived as a church, finished up as a secular mausoleum. The leader of the National Constituent Assembly ordered the change of use in 1791 as a place of interment for celebrated intellectuals and famous French citizens.[17] As we walked around the crypt, we saw monuments in memory of Voltaire, Rousseau, and Victor Hugo to name a few.

After leaving the Panthéon, we walked to the cathedral of Notre-Dame. The church was completed during the middle of the fourteenth century and the impressive structure is a perfect example of French Gothic architecture. The cathedral, situated on a natural island on the Seine River, is accessible from many historic bridges crossing the river. The French call the island *Île de la Cité* and its history dates back to medieval times. Many historical events took place within the church: the marriage of Mary Queen of Scots in 1558 to the French Dauphin Francis, the coronation of the Emperor Napoleon 1 and Victor Hugo set his novel, *The Hunchback of Notre-Dame* in the cathedral.

By the time we had finished our tour of the magnificent cathedral, it was well past lunchtime. We found a café for lunch and took the Metro once again to Montmartre. The area is famous for its white-domed basilica Sacré-Coeur. The church crowns the Paris skyline and is visible across

---

[17] Antonina Vallentin and E. W. Dickes. 1948. *Mirabeau: Voice of the Revolution*. London: Hamish Hamilton. pp. 496-97, 522.

the central city. The area to the rear of the basilica is famous for street artists and is a magnet for tourists. When we arrived, we found a small pavement café looking out on to an open cobbled stone plaza. Pedestrians were musing around a host of wooden easels, admiring the work of Bohemian street artists. The crowds of tourists mingled with the multitude of mounted canvases displaying white chalk and charcoal drawings and colourful oil paintings.

For lunch, we each chose to eat an open baguette, filled with ripe Camembert cheese and indulged in our love of beer, ordering *deux français bières veuillez,* cold from the tap. When we had finished our food, we wanted another beer. We ordered two more – we were on holiday. The conversation predictably turned towards our initial impressions of Paris and its people, compared with the worldview of France shaped by our ethnocentric teachers from our schooldays.

I recall when studying the Middle Ages, our history teacher used the Hundred Years War surreptitiously to exploit our sense of nationalism. When examining famous battles, the focus was on victories achieved by the English against the French. Crécy, Agincourt and the execution of Joan of Arc in Rouen in 1431 were prime examples, with little consideration for the French perspective.

The glorification of war, particularly where the French were involved, influenced our young hearts and minds, leaving us with a sense of animosity towards the French. English success in battles over the centuries created a worldview of the French as the natural enemy - this view we had learnt at school was now being tested partly because we found the individuals we met during our visit just as engaging as our fellow countrymen. The experience impressed deeply on us the error of judging people within a nation by their collective ethnicity alone.

By the middle of the week we realised our funds would not last the week. We were spending far too much money on food and drink, as well as entrance fees to the places we visited. Before we left England, we had naively underestimated our expenditure. The reality was we would have to leave our *pension* on Thursday morning if we were going to pay our account in full. Budgeting was not our forte.

The only solution was to access further funds. However, the question was where from? On the Wednesday night, we had visited a district named Quartier Pigalle. Famous during World War II, soldiers on leave often frequented this area. The district had a reputation for its raunchy nightlife. Along the main boulevard is the Place Pigalle, where the cabaret Moulin Rouge is situated. Famous for its nude shows, the venue was expensive and way above our budget. As we continued walking along the Boulevard de Clichy, we passed many performing street artists, entertaining passing tourists.

One in particular was a juggler. The act required him to eat light bulbs, or that's how it came over to the crowd. The illusion the artist performed was amazing and resulted in passers-by placing a few coins in a hat in appreciation. In the side streets running off the crowded boulevard, scantily clad prostitutes overtly plied their trade in the shadows. Many ladies of the night encouraged their potential clients with eye-catching expressions of encouragement and called out uncouth invitations to engage in sex.

We had not eaten since lunchtime, but we were ready for another drink. We turned off the main thoroughfare and walked down Rue Pigalle, renowned for its jazz clubs and intimate bars. One establishment in particular attracted our attention. Its small frontage opened out directly onto the street, the windows were open, and the wooden louvre shutters that usually protected the glass were folded back. The entrance was via a small doorway on the left. Looking inside, from the dimly lit shadowy pavement, the bar was packed with patrons. Behind them was a boisterous jazz trio silhouetted against the dim smoky yellow lights of the bar. The ensemble comprised a pianist in dark jeans and tee shirt playing a small grand piano and dressed in similar attire were the other two musicians playing a double bass and clarinet.

The name of the venue was Fred Payne's Bar. Later we discovered the bar was reputed to be the setting chosen by Henry Millar for his celebrated novel, *Black Spring*.[18] We entered and sat on circular high stools scattered along the frontage of the long zinc bar. The crowd was indifferent to our arrival and we decided to order something different. Instead of our usual choice of beer, we made a fatal mistake. We ordered two glasses of Green Chartreuse, a French liqueur with an alcohol content of 55%. This regrettable decision proved to be our undoing. However, it did provide the impetus for focusing our minds; where and how were we were going to access funds for our remaining time in Paris.

As the evening wore on, we became more and more intoxicated. I suddenly had a *dazzling* idea. I looked directly at Robert and said, 'Why don't we go and talk to someone at the British Embassy? Isn't that what the embassy is for – to help and assist distressed British citizens when they are away overseas?'

Robert was less adventurous. He replied, 'I'm not sure that's such a good idea,' without explaining his reason for thinking so.

'What other options do we have?' I said, slurring my speech and attempting to push my empty glass towards the barman, indicating I wanted another glass of Chartreuse.

---

[18] Henry Miller. *Black Spring*, New York: Grove Press, 1963, p. 215.

'We could contact my parents and see what they could do,' Robert suggested, his tone expressing no genuine enthusiasm to do so.

I did not take Robert's suggestion seriously. My attention was preoccupied by my original idea; what other choice did we really have? It seemed the only viable way forward to resolve our dilemma. To be honest, the effect of the alcohol certainly contributed to my confidence in the scheme. It was time to leave Fred Payne's. We slowly staggered back to our hotel during the early hours of Thursday morning. The only solution to our financial concerns was nothing other than to proceed, as we really had no alternative.

When we woke up later that morning, we felt confident with the decision we had made. It must have been our young bodies; neither of us felt any affects from the excess liquor and we didn't suffer a hangover. We packed our cases, paid our account at the desk and left the Rue La Boétie, heading towards the British Embassy a few blocks away.

The imposing embassy building is on Rue du Faubourg Saint-Honoré. We arrived carrying our cases and I briefly explained our circumstances to a person staffing the reception desk, who asked us to wait for someone who could assist us.

A few minutes later, a middle-aged, well-dressed woman greeted us in the reception area. She led us down an imposing corridor to a small meeting room. Inside was the mandatory gilded framed photograph of Queen Elizabeth on the wall. Once seated, we explained we had run out of funds, having seriously underestimated our expenditure. She asked us when we were travelling home to Britain and I explained we had air tickets to travel home that Saturday.

She asked us for our passports and reminded us soberly that it is essential to have sufficient funds, when travelling abroad, in the event of an emergency. I explained we had made a serious error of judgement and apologised profusely for the inconvenience we were causing. To our relief, she accepted our explanation without further scrutiny. Robert and I could not believe our good luck.

She announced in a formal manner that we would receive the French equivalent of twenty pounds each (then equivalent to an average weeks' pay in 1965.) The sense of relief we both felt would have been clearly evident on our faces, as we expressed our gratitude. Her official demeanour softened with a friendly smile as she wrote out a requisition enabling us to access the agreed funds. We signed an agreement, acknowledging the advance of funds was repayable and our passport would be subject to surrender by Customs on arrival in England. When the loan had been paid, our passports would be returned. As we left the meeting room, we were instructed to follow her to the cashier's office to obtain the funds. Having accepted the money, we thanked her again and left the building.

Our first task was to search for cheaper accommodation. We were both energised by our good fortune, knowing we would be able to continue enjoying our vacation. I looked at our map and we decided to head eastwards. Eventually we came across a long narrow street, Rue St-Denis, leading down towards the River Seine. One of the oldest streets in Paris, it traces its origins to the 1st century when the Romans occupied the area. Many of the side streets leading off the main thoroughfare contained a variety of small inexpensive *pension* type lodgings.

Although the area was rundown, it gave us a wide insight into Bohemian Paris. Once we had found a suitable place to stay, we left our cases with the proprietor and prudently paid our accommodation costs upfront.

We walked down towards the river, heading right along the embankment. After a few minutes, we arrived at the Musée du Louvre. Almost every visitor to Paris wants to see the *Mona Lisa* by Leonardo da Vinci and we were no exception.

Our last few days in Paris passed too quickly. Predominantly our focus was on eating and drinking, sometimes to excess. We were young and carefree, determined to enjoy the rest of the time we had left. Both the journey to Paris and the time we spent together opened up a new worldview. We began to appreciate that each individual is autonomous and each person has to overcome the challenges of life on their own terms, in their own unique way.

***

1959 to 1965 was the period of my adolescent years. The velocity of change in hindsight was bewildering and the visit to France had given me the opportunity to reflect and to some extent, escape facing reality. Comparing new horizons to my own situation at home made me reflect more on the dynamics of identity and my ethnicity. I began to question the eternal argument, between the rights of the individual, versus the wider claim of society. That dichotomy between individualism and collectivism led me to think more about my own identity as an individual. Unfortunately, at the time I suppressed my inclination to find out more about my past. I was unable to find the inner strength to discuss my feelings with Mum and Dad concerning my adoption. The fear and shame I felt inside was stronger than the desire to learn more of my origins. You can run away but you can't hide; I chose to adhere to the former.

Earlier, I referred to the assertion of wishing to travel which I found compelling. Although I was searching for something, I didn't consciously connect the desire to travel with the suppressed search for identity. I had a strong sense of wanting to discover my own ethnicity and my genealogical origins, but I was unable to actually do it.

Many adopted children are unable to discuss and explore their concerns for fear of distressing their adoptive parents. Some children may suppress this inclination because they believe that if they inquire too forcefully, they may be rejected and are unable to manage the potential anger expressed by their adoptive parents. The fear of abandonment is overwhelming.

Reflecting back, I recall how strong that sense of confusion was and that there was a key component of me, which was missing. Not being conscious of what I was seeking, I naturally didn't know where to find it. One scholar, H. J. Sants, describes this phenomenon as "genealogical bewilderment".[19] Sants claims an adopted child who has little or no knowledge of his natural parents, is fundamentally insecure, which may affect their mental health.[20] Many children become preoccupied with the idea of finding their biological parent and for some this becomes an obsession, believing that in finding a solution to the problem, all their difficulties will be resolved.[21] Perhaps inadvertently I used the opportunity to *travel* as a diversion from investigating my biological origins. The suppressed sense of shame I felt about my predicament, overpowered taking any other action. The dilemma on how to resolve the problem would have to wait longer.

---

[19] H. J. Sants. "Genealogical Bewilderment in Children with Substitute Parents." *British Journal of Medical Psychology* 37, no. 2 (1964): p. 131.

[20] ibid, p. 131.

[21] ibid, p. 131.

Chapter 7

The weekend following our return home from Paris was set aside to celebrate our engagement. Judy's parents generously hosted the reception at their home. The weather in August is often unpredictable and that year was no exception. Luckily, the Saturday we chose turned out to be hot and sultry. Mum and Dad joined Judy's relatives; my sister Monica was notably absent. Dad extended sincere apologies to Judy's parents without submitting a convincing reason.

The function started around four thirty in the afternoon and finished before eight o'clock. Judy and her sister were dressed in brightly coloured pink dresses. Their mother was an accomplished seamstress and made the twins' dresses especially for the occasion. Both girls had backcombed hairstyles, held in place with copious amounts of hair lacquer. The fashion at the time was for young women to wear flattering six-inch high-heeled shoes. My future wife and sister-in-law were no exception.

Those who attended were split by gender; the front living room of the small semi-detached was full of men and a lounge-cum-dining room at the back of the house became the exclusive domain of the women. The only exception to the division of the sexes was Judy's mother Dora and her husband Bill. They were transient, constantly carrying plates of sandwiches, sausage rolls, and cakes from the kitchen to the guests.

Drinks were Bill's domain and by inclination, he disliked hosting parties. A quiet and generous man, he preferred male company, one to one. Being a straightforward and practical man he felt uncomfortable when people grouped together just to exchange pleasantries and engage in polite conversation. Alcoholic drinks were restricted to beer for the men and sweet sherry for mature women in the group. Younger females at the party, including Judy and her sister Janet, drank white wine. For my part, I stuck to beer, as did Janet's fiancé Albert. Many of the older adults preferred to drink more tea than alcohol and Mum and Dad predictably were no exception.

There were no speeches during the gathering. Judy and I received many generous engagement presents, focused on our perceived future needs: bathroom scales, small kitchen appliances, numerous towels and the like. Conversation between the adults was limited to polite exchanges and I sensed a general unease between Mum and Dad and Judy's parents, shaped by their perceived disparity in social class.

The party had no music although Judy and Janet possessed a Dansette record player, a must-have for all teenagers at the time. There was no dancing or laughter as there should have been. The tone of the function was to please the older generation. We did what was expected; we behaved in a manner acceptable to our elders.

***

One day during August 1965, I attended a special meeting with my boss Peter Kirkby. The purpose was to discuss an opportunity to work away from Birmingham. Peter explained the company, which had many offices throughout the United Kingdom, had experienced staff difficulties within one of their facilities in Scotland. The previous Friday the majority of the staff working at the company's Prestwick office, had resigned. Those leaving included the core management team. Their motive was to launch a new business venture in direct opposition to their former employer. These unexpected events necessitated in bringing together a small team of specialist staff from offices throughout Britain and relocating them to Scotland.

'Would you like to live and work in Scotland?' Peter said. 'The job's based at Prestwick Airport, right on the Ayrshire coast. It would be a great opportunity for you!'

'How long would I be there for?'

'At this stage, we envisage a six month secondment. The company will pay for your travel to and from Scotland, as well as providing accommodation and meals during your stay.'

I accepted the job with enthusiasm, seeing it as a great adventure. Time was of the essence, so after returning to the Birmingham airport office, I told Judy the decision I had taken. Judy was very supportive of my decision and when I told her I would return home every third week, she saw the job as a stepping-stone to gaining future promotion.

I travelled home to tell Mum the exciting news. Surprisingly Mum welcomed the idea. Seeing it as a fantastic short-term opportunity, she thought the appointment would give me the chance to broaden my work experience, as well as live in a new environment.

'I'll be home every month,' I told her. 'I have to fly out tonight.'

'That soon? What did Judy say?' she asked. 'She must have been very surprised.'

'She was,' I said. 'It came right out of the blue – It's a real chance for both of us.'

'Dad and I will miss you. When will you be home again?'

'Hopefully in four to five weeks Mum,' I said reassuringly.

Dad was at work and I needed to pack and leave home before five. Mum ironed my shirts for me and I gathered my things together and closed my suitcase.

'Tell Dad I'll phone him tomorrow from Scotland,' I said as I went to kiss Mum goodbye.

I placed my suitcase in my Mini and waved Mum goodbye. When I arrived at Birmingham airport, I left my car locked outside the office car park. An hour later, I flew out heading for Glasgow.

When I arrived at Glasgow Airport, it was late at night. Ian Stewart, the manager of the Glasgow office, met me and drove me to the central city. My room for the night was booked at St Enoch's hotel in the central city. The following morning we both travelled by car to Prestwick Airport and a new adventure had begun. Once past the Firth of Clyde, we drove through the upper part of Ayrshire. The scenery looked very different compared to the English countryside. Much of the landscape was moorland used for open grazing and many of the fields were much larger than I expected. The open stony terrain, scattered with bracken and heather, supported fewer cattle and sheep than English lowland farming, and the character of the land was far more rustic.

Our journey to Prestwick went through Kilmarnock, a small town famous for the Johnnie Walker whisky distillery. We arrived at the airport well before lunch. After exchanging introductions between the few staff members who had remained from the previous week, I met some of the new team on secondment like myself. After Ian Stewart left to return to Glasgow, Ian Goldie, the local manager, called the team together. He set about explaining to us our individual tasks and I spent the rest of the day coming to grips with the new challenges ahead of me.

My first day at Prestwick turned out to be a long one. Shortly after five, I left the office with a colleague, who like me, had travelled from another city. David lived in London and we were booked in at the same digs. The walk from the airport to our new abode along Monkton Road was the main thoroughfare leading to the township of Prestwick. The guesthouse was a two storey terraced house, built from local stone with a sombre grey slate roof. We approached the Victorian frontage facing the busy main road. I rang the entrance bell and a middle-aged woman opened the door.

'Hello, I'm Mrs McGuire, welcome to Ayrshire. You two must be Paul and David – welcome to you both,' she said, in a soft Scottish brogue.

We responded to her greeting and entered the hallway.

'Your company told me you would be with us for a while. Is this your first time in Scotland?' she asked, addressing us both.

'It is for me,' said David.

'Me too,' I replied. 'I'm really looking forward to it.'

Mrs McGuire handed us our room keys. 'I'll show you your rooms – just follow me please,' she said, briskly leading the way upstairs.

We picked up our suitcases and climbed the creaking wooden stairway leading to the second floor. As we stood outside our bedroom doors, Mrs McGuire stood in the corridor and looked directly at us.

'Dinner is at six-thirty sharp in the dining room downstairs and please remember, there's no smoking in the bedrooms boys, but you can smoke downstairs,' she declared, with a less amiable look on her face.

Leaving us to our own devices, she turned towards the stairway. 'I hope you both enjoy your stay with us.'

After she had left, I turned to David. 'Let's meet downstairs just before dinner – we'd better not be late!'

158

'See you later, I hope the food's OK – I'm starving,' David concurred with a grin, as we entered our sleeping quarters.

I closed my door. Inside was a reminder of Mrs McGuire's instructions, a no-smoking sign in bold red lettering was fixed above a large mirror.

My room contained a single bed. The headboard faced the mirror and the bed was covered with a patchwork quilt eiderdown, embroidered in light grey and pastel green. I noticed immediately there was no bedside light, probably to save on electricity. I thought to myself, the Scottish always had a reputation for frugal living. To read comfortably required reliance on a single bulb, hanging from a high central ceiling rose. The wide brim lampshade was covered in cream brocade had gold tassels hanging around the edge. Two narrow bottle green rugs lay on both sides of the bed and the rest of the floor displayed black stained floorboards, which contrasted against a high-edged skirting board, painted cream.

A small chest of draws and a wardrobe to match were the only furniture in the room, except for a single sturdy Chippendale chair. The seat finished with elaborate tracery, stood next to the single bay window and looked like a low-cost reproduction. The bedroom had no en-suite. A bleak sign on the back of the door advised guests that bathrooms were available along the corridor outside. The view from the window looked out to the windswept Irish Sea. Beyond, when the weather was clear, it was possible to see the Isle of Arran and even the coastline of Northern Ireland.

The dinner we ate that evening was less than spectacular to say the least. A thin minestrone soup was followed by a main course of minced beef with mashed potato and carrots covered in rich gravy. For desert, we had apple crumble with thick custard. In itself, it was wholesome enough, but as the days turned into weeks, the variety of the menu remained uninspiring - and I am being more than generous.

After dinner, to reduce the monotony and tedium of the evenings, David and I would often meet other colleagues from work at one of the local pubs in the small township. Our choice of drinks was a pint of *heavy* beer unlike the bitter more popular in England. Although locals kept to themselves, many engaged in conversation, detecting from our accents we were Sassenachs from south of the border. Often we would play darts in the bar. The drinks were cheaper there and occasionally we would splash out and enjoy a Scotch whisky on the side, as was the local custom.

The social culture in Scotland was very different to England. In particular, the Scots were proud of their identity as evidenced by their unique surnames. Many Scots derive their origin from clans. The word comes from *clanna*, the Gaelic for children. Over time, the requirement to claim ancestry on descent has changed. Territory determined clan allegiance and those who lived within it, adhered to the authority of the clan chief. Many surnames with the prefix Mac, as in Mackinnon or MacDonald indicate to which clan an individual belongs.

During my time in Scotland, I had plenty of free time to think. The public display of ethnicity influenced me deeply. The demonstrative attention and loyalty Scots displayed towards clan and kinship was something I had not experienced before. The question as to my own identity and ethnicity was still unanswered and unresolved. My visit to Scotland reinforced my sense of insecurity further. I still did not know *who* I really was.

I flew back home every month as planned. I spent Christmas 1965, with both Judy and my family in Birmingham. I decided to drive back to Scotland and spend the New Year in Prestwick. It gave me an opportunity to experience Hogmanay. This traditional Scottish celebration is very different from New Year celebrations in England.

Unlike the English, festivities do not start early in the evening on the last day of the year. People in Scotland go about their normal business during the hours prior to midnight and only begin to start their celebrating a few minutes before the clock strikes the midnight hour. Festivities then commence. It was unusual for me, but I had taken the opportunity of purchasing a bottle of Scotch whisky earlier that evening, just in case I felt like indulging later with some vigour. I discovered that many people continue celebrating until the early daylight hours of New Year's Day. I went out first footing, taking the bottle of whisky with me, as I knocked on neighbours' doors to share a wee dram. I immersed myself in the traditional activities and was somewhat the worse for wear after festivities ended.

A few weeks after having returned to work in January 1966, I began to think more carefully about what my next career move would be. Following the end of my secondment to Prestwick, my expectation was I would be returning from Scotland to my previous job in Birmingham. Living away from home had widened my expectations. I began to search the trade papers, looking for new opportunities and I came across an advertisement seeking a Cargo Sales Representative for Trans World Airlines based in London. That night I put pen to paper and included my CV with my covering letter. On the way to work the following morning I slipped the letter in to the post-box outside the local shop.

It must have been at least ten days before I heard anything further. One evening as David and I were waiting for our evening meal, Mrs McGregor came up briskly to our table.

'Paul – There's a letter that came for you today – I've left it for you in the mail tray in the hallway.'

'Thanks Mrs McGregor,' I replied, excusing myself from the table. I walked into the hallway to retrieve the letter. The envelope bore a central London postmark. I slipped the unopened correspondence into my inside jacket pocket and returned to our table.

As I sat down, David looked up, 'Anything interesting?'

'I haven't opened it yet – Looks like it's from Judy. I'll open it later,' I said, knowing he would not ask any further questions on a letter from my fiancée. As we continued eating our dinner, I knew I would have to tell David if I was successful in gaining an interview. Although we were both enjoying our time in Scotland, we had discussed on various occasions what we would do when our secondment finished. We both hoped that the work experience in Prestwick would result in promotion. Deep down though, we realised that to gain advancement, we needed to become more proactive.

When we had finished our dinner, I said to David, 'I think I'll turn in early tonight. I have some reading to do and I'd better reply to Judy's letter.' He readily accepted my explanation and we bade each other good night.

As soon as I had closed the bedroom door, I tore open the envelope. It was as I suspected, from TWA. The letter thanked me for my application and asked me to attend an interview at their office in London's West End. During my lunch break the following morning, I found a telephone booth in the airport passenger terminal and arranged an appointment on the second Wednesday in February at two o'clock.

I decided to take a week's vacation, commencing at the end of that week. Fortunately, my boss was happy for me to take a week's holiday. I booked a flight back home for the coming Saturday and then rang Judy to tell her I would be flying back to Birmingham.

Immediately after I had arrived at Birmingham Airport, I drove to meet Judy at her parents' house. I showed her the letter I had received from TWA, as well as the job advertisement. She took an optimistic view and saw the opportunity as being mutually beneficial. Judy had one major concern.

'Do you think you'll get the job Paul? It does sound exciting.'

'I don't know – I really want the job – it would change our lives!' I said.

'It would mean living in London,' Judy said regretfully.

'I'd get digs in London and every weekend I'd come back to Birmingham.'

We had planned to get married in March of the following year. Our hearts were set on buying a new house in the Midlands. Changing jobs would put a different perspective on our dreams. Housing in the London area was much more expensive and typically, I hadn't given the matter as much thought, as it deserved.

'How would we be able to afford a house if we lived in London?' Judy asked.

'I haven't got the job yet,' I said attempting to avert her concern. 'Let's see how the interview goes and what the prospects are likely to be.'

Later that afternoon we drove over to see Mum and Dad who were both glad to see us. Initially when I arrived home, they thought my visit was one of my three weekly stopovers. I told Mum and Dad about the new opportunity. Predictably, Dad thought it was far too soon to change employers and Mum was of a similar opinion. I knew there was no point in trying to convince them of the merits of the job in London. The best approach was to proceed with the interview and see what the outcome would deliver. If the interview was successful, I would be able to present a more convincing argument to appease them. I spent the rest of the weekend with Judy and returned home on Sunday evening.

I left by car for central London early on Wednesday morning. Taking the motorway, the journey to central London took less than two hours. I parked my car in a multi-storey car park close to Oxford Circus. Dressed in my only dark grey business suit, I grabbed a quick sandwich for lunch, and continued walking to my scheduled meeting at two o'clock.

The TWA office was located in Duke Street. The entrance was directly opposite a side entrance to Selfridges, a large departmental store in central Oxford Street. I gave my name to the receptionist who asked me to wait. Within a few minutes Mr Barnett, a tall middle-aged man dressed in a light grey herringbone suit introduced himself. He wore what looked like expensive spectacles, had well groomed grey silver hair, and sported a distinguished grey moustache, twisted at each end. We briefly shook hands. He then invited me to follow him to his office on the second floor.

The interview itself took no longer than forty minutes. As the meeting drew to a close, Mr Barnett said he would let me know the outcome within a few days. I got up from my seat and said goodbye, while he remained seated behind his desk. Just before I opened the door, Mr Barnett asked me to return back to my seat. Somewhat surprised I sat down.

He looked me straight in the eye and said. 'Paul – this may appear strange to you, but I wanted to look at the heels of your shoes as you walked towards the door. I believe, if a person maintains his shoes well and the heels are not worn down on the edges, this reflects the character of the owner.'

To my amazement, he immediately offered me the position, subject to receiving a satisfactory reference from my current employer. After a brief discussion on terms and conditions, I gratefully accepted. The meeting closed, I said my farewell once again, shook his hand and left the office elated with the outcome.

When I arrived back home, Mum and Dad were amazed to hear the good news. Dad muttered some comment about, 'some people have all the luck and just continually keep landing on their feet.'

I phoned Judy to tell her the news and returned to Scotland at the weekend. She was elated at my good fortune as it provided an improve salary package with good prospects. The downside was we would be apart again, except for weekends when I would travel back to Birmingham.

***

I left my job at Prestwick during the last week of March 1966 and started work in London at the beginning of April. My new job involved travelling throughout Britain, visiting freight forwarding agencies and large commercial organisations. The purpose was to secure clients' shipping goods by airfreight to and from the United States. At the time, the airfreight business was in its infancy.

The position involved entertaining clients and the sales team enjoyed a generous expense allowance. The airline business was doing well and employees were well paid. To my surprise, my expense account exceeded my salary. The industry from an outside perspective projected the image of luxury and the good life in exotic locations. From the very beginning, I began to enjoy extensive travel, combined with good hotels, not to mention an introduction to memorable restaurants, often in the company of interesting people.

I had arranged lodgings in London through the auspices of one of Dad's London friends. The house was in a small two-storey Victorian terrace in Tulse Hill, south London. Tenants had their own sparsely furnished room. I first arrived at the house during daylight hours; all the front windows were covered in dreary faded curtains. My room featured a single bed, an uncomfortable chair, a small electric cooker, and a sink with hot and cold running water. Above the sink bench was an inefficient gas fired water heater. The house and its location were bleak. During April, the weather was still cold at night. Fortunately, my room also had a small gas room-heater. Both gas appliances were monitored by an individual meter, with a voracious appetite. It demanded regular feeding with shilling coins to allow the gas to flow. Electricity consumption was controlled by a sub meter and the cost was recoverable later by the landlord from each tenant.

After three weeks, I had had enough of Tulse Hill. The house had a small bathroom with a shower used by all the occupants. The water heater in the bathroom also needed coins to operate. I took my shower in the mornings and to allow the steam from the shower to dissipate, it was essential to leave the window ajar, as the room had no extractor.

The view from the window faced onto a cemetery and crematorium. Although this was not the reason I left, it did not engender an optimistic outlook so early in the morning. During my stay in Tulse Hill, I never met any other tenant. I would travel back from the office in central London, open the front door, and climb the stairway leading to my room. After having placed a few mandatory coins in the meter, I would then set about preparing a simple meal. The digs were so miserable I would retire early to bed.

At the end of my third week, Richard, an old friend from Birmingham, rang me at work. He suggested driving over to my place on Saturday morning to catch up and see how I was faring in south London. He arrived mid-morning and within ten minutes suggested, I pack my bags and move into his flat. Richard shared the apartment, which was north of the River Thames, with two other flatmates and the

166

location was much better. I jumped at the opportunity; all I needed was a little mild persuasion.

I notified the landlord that I was vacating. Fortunately, he resided in the same street I was leaving. Having tidied my room, I gave him back the house keys and placed my meagre belongings in the boot of Richard's car. Luckily, the rent was only payable one week in advance and no bond had been required. The cost of exit was the least of my problems.

Richard's apartment had an impressive address: Wymering Mansions, Wymering Road, Maida Vale. The drive from south London to Maida Vale took less than forty minutes. Richard parked outside. We climbed the six steep flights of stairs to the third floor carrying my belongings with us. The Edwardian tenement block possessed no elevator and by the time we reached Richard's front door, we were both exhausted.

The rooms inside the apartment were spacious and had high ceilings. It had four bedrooms and Richard helped me with my luggage to my room. It was the epitome of a bachelor apartment. The spacious lounge looked out through a curved bay window and onto the road below. Furnished with a large settee were two armchairs, originally from Richard's parents. The used ashtrays were in need of cleaning and the room was in disarray. Littered on the floor or strewn on chairs, were old newspapers and magazines. A wide corridor connected through to the hallway, leading onto the landing adjacent to the stairwell. It provided access to the bedrooms, as well as to a large combined kitchen and dining room. Adjacent to the kitchen was a small bathroom needing refurbishment. The bedrooms all had second-hand single beds, all of which only provided the minimum utility and comfort. The lounge and bedrooms were all fitted with stained beige wall-to-wall carpeting and some areas needed replacing. For the rest there was little other furniture. The exception was a large wooden kitchen table and assorted chairs and in each bedroom was a second-hand chest of draws.

The most important appliance in the apartment was the refrigerator. I soon learned its essential purpose was not only for keeping food fresh, but storing cheap wine and beer. All of us considered the refrigerator an essential item to our wellbeing, although it was never kept very clean. The only other appliance was a washing machine, but it was not in working order. We made our own arrangements to wash clothes at a local launderette.

Like me, all the flatmates had fulltime jobs and lived busy lives. We rarely socialised outside the confines of the apartment, as we had our own circle of friends. Richard and I did meet up occasionally, but all of us were engaged in developing our own careers in different industries.

During the year I lived at Wymering Mansions, I travelled back to Birmingham most weekends. Judy and I planned to get married in the spring of 1967 and chose the 4th of March as our big day. As time progressed, we began to think more seriously about where we would live. Our preference was to live reasonably close to London. My job was progressing well and we both saw a future together in the prosperous South East of England. Like many young couples, we found it expensive to buy close to London. Eventually we placed a deposit on a two-bedroom bungalow, fifty-miles west from the centre of London. This house was one of the only places we could find that was affordable; the downside was I had a long distance to commute.

Our wedding took place in a Franciscan Monastery. The decision to have a Catholic wedding ceremony was to some extent to appease Mum and Dad. Judy came from a Protestant background and at the time, to marry in a Catholic church, we both had to agree to bring up any children from the marriage as Catholics. Reflecting back, that decision was very one sided. In particular, Judy was more than generous in agreeing to that demand and little regard was given to how my future in-laws would feel about the obligation. The decisions we entered into were not Judy's and mine; we merely accepted the established social conventions and expectations of my parents.

The weather turned out well on the big day and many friends and family filled the church. My best man was my brother-in-law Albert. Judy's twin sister Janet and my sister Monica were bridesmaids. Judy had insisted that her local Anglican priest should be present at the ceremony, which was considered at the time most unusual. Interfaith practices between different denominations were not encouraged.

After the reception, we both left by car and drove to the Cotswolds. I can recall how I felt as we both climbed into our car and set off for the short drive to our honeymoon hotel. Judy was radiant and dressed in a very attractive two-piece suit and as we turned towards each other and kissed, I knew I had made the right decision to marry such a wonderful woman.

We had both chosen a small country hotel in a beautiful village near Cheltenham. Our original intention was to have a holiday in Greece, but decided to put all our available funds into financing our new home. In hindsight, we should have splashed out. We were both conservative in nature and the idea of two weeks in Greece enjoying each other in the sun just seemed far too extravagant. After returning from our honeymoon, we moved to our new bungalow in Berkshire.

***

A few weeks after settling into our new home, I left London for New York. TWA had its Training Academy based at John F Kennedy airport and I left for two weeks to participate in a sales and marketing course. My only overseas trip had been to Paris and flying to New York first class in a Boeing 707 was exciting. There was no business class in those days, it was either first or economy. The accommodation was less extravagant, a comfortable motel close to the airport, where many other trainees were staying.

My first impression of the United States was of a land of plenty. What struck me in particular was the conspicuous wealth of the elite and many of the middle class. In stark contrast, there was a poor underclass, mainly citizens of African and Hispanic descent, who generally worked in menial and blue-collar occupations. Yet, those I met had an outward demeanour of infectious enthusiasm. Their general tone of conversation expressed a sense of optimism towards life. The key objective of most Americans seemed to be a preoccupation in attaining an ever-greater standard of living. The pursuit of the mighty dollar and conspicuous consumption were paramount to the popular ideal of the *good life*.

Compared with the general population in Britain, my view gained from a New York perspective, was that many Americans appeared to eat more, dress better and drive large powerful motor vehicles and fuel efficiency was not even a consideration as petroleum at the pump was cheap. Six or eight cylinder vehicles were the order of the day, unlike the smaller powered engines fitted in the majority of cars sold in Britain. For those who had a job, there was more disposable income compared to Britain. The biggest contrast I saw between the two nations was the American sense of optimism; it seemed anything was possible.

America, in 1966 was still a nation at war. The Vietnam conflict had been going on since 1956 and conscription for military service was the norm. Following the assassination of John F Kennedy in November 1963, Vice-President Lyndon B Johnson became President. The legacy of the Kennedy years and the spirit of optimism still lingered on in America and beyond. The United States was the world's superpower and the predicted eclipse from western to eastern political power had yet to crystallise as an idea in the public imagination.

Yet for many young people in the United States, a counter-culture grew, advocating social change. Built on a legacy from the 1950's and extending into 1960's, a generation began to challenge the conservatism and social norms of the period. The experience of the Vietnam War and the Cold War between East and West encouraged the younger generation to demand a more liberated society. That social dynamic was very apparent when talking with young people in New York. Many of the people I met had come to live in New York, either from other states, or from overseas. It was a vibrant melting pot of different ethnicities, charged with possibilities.

Leading on from the Civil Rights movement, the focus in the USA shifted towards environmental concerns. The process was often driven with a feminist perspective and gender politics were the topic of conversation amidst the sexual revolution. This change was often expressed by the young through their distinctive long hair and rock music culture.[22] During 1967, the world would see these ideas expressed in the Summer of Love, an innovative social phenomenon held in San Francisco. The event celebrated hippie culture and exposed to a wider audience the use of psychedelic drugs and free love. This was practiced by many young people, uniting them together in a common cause.[23]

---

[22] Wikipedia contributors, "History of the United States (1964–80)," *Wikipedia, The Free Encyclopedia,* http://en.wikipedia.org/w/index.php?title=History_of_the_United_States_(196 4%E2%80%9380)&oldid=599335995 (accessed May 15, 2014).

[23] Wikipedia contributors, "History of the United States (1964–80)," *Wikipedia, The Free Encyclopedia,*

***

My job in London continued to go well and in the September of 1967, I relocated back to the Midlands. Ironically, Birmingham Airport was again my base. This suited Judy, as she was closer to her family. For me, returning to the Midlands made business travel throughout Britain far more convenient. We sold our first home and purchased a new detached house a few miles outside Warwick.

Shortly after moving into our new home, Judy fell pregnant. We were both thrilled with the news, as were both sets of parents. The baby was due in the summer of 1968 and our first child Nicola was born on the 17th of June. The birth process had been difficult and finally the medical team decided on performing a caesarean. Fathers were prohibited from visiting their partner in hospital. This extended even to their new-born child. The reason given at the time was concerns about potential infections.

I first saw my wonderful baby daughter through an outside window of the maternity ward. I had phoned the ward and spoken to Judy and we arranged a time and location for a nurse to bring baby Nicola to a window for me to catch my first glimpse of her. When I saw her face and tiny fingers, I was overwhelmed. How beautiful and perfect she was. I became aware of a strange feeling; this was the first time I had ever seen a blood relation, my own flesh and blood.

As the weeks progressed, Judy quickly recovered from the trauma of the surgery and Nicola grew from strength to strength. She became the apple of my eye and my thoughts

http://en.wikipedia.org/w/index.php?title=History_of_the_United_States_(196 4%E2%80%9380)&oldid=599335995 (accessed May 15, 2014).

once again turned to my unfulfilled longing to find out more about my origins. Having a young baby, as well focusing on turning our new house into a home, was Judy's and my first priority. During this period of my life, I again avoided taking any concrete steps to tracing my own ancestry, pushing the idea further to the back of my mind.

Our second child was born in June 1971. Like Nicola, Matthew was also cherished as an equally special gift. Judy was fortunate in having a normal birth with our only son and as our two children entered their early childhood years, we got on and enjoyed family life together. Judy's twin sister lived close to where we lived. This gave us the perfect opportunity for both families to share those early childhood years and Janet's two young boys, as well as the grandparents from both our families spent many happy times together.

In June 1973 the family celebrated Matthew's second birthday and Nicola's fifth. Our children were quite different in temperament, yet their family phenotype was easily distinguishable. We were fortunate our home was in a village surrounded by beautiful Warwickshire countryside. Often we would go for walks in the country lanes. I remember fondly how Nicola loved to walk with Judy and me among the late springtime bluebells growing wild in the nearby woodlands. Our short time living in Warwick was a happy one and we made many friends. Unfortunately, times were changing on the economic and political front, which would have a major bearing on our future.

***

In Britain, the winter of 1973 proved to be a winter of discontent. Industrial unrest compounded the economic woes of the nation. The coal miners' strike in 1972 that strove for higher wages, followed by further industrial action by miners in early 1974, brought about the government ordering a three-day working week affecting many industries. Essential industries received electric power. Many people who were required to work a three-day week received reduced wages. To conserve energy, most people were subject to reduced electricity supply. Industrial action by miner's pickets at the gates of power stations halted coal supplies reaching the generators. Old people were vulnerable in their homes to unpredictable power outages and the government of Edward Heath eventually called a general election in February 1974, attempting to obtain a mandate to resist the miners' demands.

Heath's response failed and the result of the elections was a hung parliament. After his defeat, he attempted to forge an alliance with the Liberal Party but was unsuccessful. The mêlée subsequently delivered a minority Labour government in February 1974, led by Harold Wilson, following Edward Heath's resignation as Prime Minister.

At the time, the international airline industry was experiencing a cyclical downturn and TWA was no exception. A few weeks prior to the government falling, I received news on the 3rd of January that my position had become redundant. I was one of over ten thousand TWA employees worldwide having to look for another job.

The industrial climate in Britain during this period was grim to say the least. I contacted many colleagues within the airline industry, but decisions to take on new staff went on hold until the outlook became clearer. Like most people facing unemployment, I did not have sufficient financial resources to sustain my outgoing mortgage commitments for more than a few weeks.

My last resort was to look for work opportunities overseas. I approached my previous employer and arranged a meeting with one of their directors in London. He suggested three overseas options: Singapore, Australia, and New Zealand. In hindsight, I should have considered them all more carefully. When I returned from the interview, Judy and I discussed the merits of each position. We both felt New Zealand was a more attractive proposition based on sentiment. The job in Singapore was a start-up role establishing the company's presence in South East Asia. Although this would have been the most challenging position, I wasn't confident enough for the challenge and Judy was reluctant about the life of an expatriate in Asia with two young children. Regarding the Australian position, we both considered living in Perth was too isolated.

We convinced ourselves the job in New Zealand was the most attractive, not just for reasons of emotion, but because it was a contract position and we could return to Britain when economic conditions improved. It seemed a safer choice and we could go back to England if things didn't work out. We didn't fully appreciate that as our lives continued, we would all put down new roots and our young children would quickly accept New Zealand as their home.

I was fortunate in being able to secure a free air ticket to Auckland through the auspices of TWA to attend an interview. I left London in mid-January and flew via Los Angeles. My itinerary allowed seven days for my round trip and I arrived in Auckland after a journey of over twenty-eight hours. At the airport, Peter, the General Manager of the New Zealand business met me and we spent the day discussing the job in detail.

The following morning I flew to Wellington. The purpose was to meet with the country director and key staff to gain a greater understanding of the role. My flight to Wellington gave me a perfect viewpoint to form an impression of the landscape and to form an appreciation of the size and scale of the country. What surprised me, looking out from the aircraft window, was the isolation of the numerous small settlements scattered below me.

This country was predominantly a rural landscape devoted to farming. Herds of cows and sheep dotted the landscape. Immigrant settlers from previous generations had laboured and cleared most suitable farmland for pasture. The diversity of the landscape with large forests, both indigenous and those planted for timber production, painted a kaleidoscope of green stretching out to the horizon. Visible from the right of the aircraft was the dark blue Tasman Sea and on the left, the vast Pacific Ocean glittered.

The topography reminded me in many ways of Ireland, where the landscape is rustic and less manicured than England. In particular, the high volcanic central plateau of the central North Island and the splendour of Mount Taranaki on the Eastern Cape confirmed Aotearoa was indeed the land of the long white cloud. This was a foreign and unfamiliar terrain and one we would shortly call our new home. I returned that evening to have dinner with Peter and his wife, at their home high up in the Waitakere Ranges close to Auckland. I left New Zealand for England a few days later with a signed offer of employment. The agreement was for three years. The contract provided gratis travel to New Zealand for the family, as well as covering the cost of shipping all our personal effects.

After returning home, we made the final decision to emigrate. Naturally, both sets of parents were shocked at our decision to relocate to Auckland. Judy's twin sister Janet was also deeply concerned at the decision we had made. The distance and remoteness of New Zealand, not to mention the cost of travel, gave them all misgivings about our decision. The only consolation for them was the three-year tenure of my contract.

Having accepted the job in Auckland, Judy and I set about making plans to leave our home in Warwickshire. I felt a sense of exhilaration, at the prospect of living in a different country, while Judy had many reservations. Judy's acceptance of the opportunity was based on the understanding that the duration of the contract was for three years. My view was that yes, the duration was for three years, but like so many things in life, circumstances change, doors close, and doors open. Neither of us really discussed how the other felt about the move. The velocity of the process, from redundancy to my starting date in Auckland, left no time to reconsider or get cold feet. We just continued with the process, went ahead, and did it.

During early February, we listed our house for sale. The market for property was in the doldrums and Judy and I agreed we would vacate the house, although we had not secured a buyer, and we left the house in the hands of estate agents. It was bitterly cold as we began the process of saying our goodbyes to friends and family. Both our young children readily accepted that we were leaving, without fully understanding the implications. In many ways, this made it easier for us, as they were supportive of this new adventure in their young lives.

Our air tickets arrived by post a few days before we were due to leave England. Seeing the tickets reinforced the reality of our forthcoming departure. The removal company scheduled all our furniture and personal belongings to be packed and shipped, as well as our only vehicle, Judy's Mini. We moved out of our house on the same day they arrived to pack and we all spent the final two days in England with Judy's twin sister and her immediate family. Separating identical twins is never an easy decision and for Judy and Janet the thought of parting was harrowing. Both girls began to feel the full impact of what our departure would mean. Those final two days were difficult for us all.

We said our goodbyes to our mums and dads. There were lots of tears and hugs and promises to meet again soon - either in England or in New Zealand. Deep down none of us really understood when we would see each other again. We all attempted to put a brave face on it. Reflecting back on those last few days before we left England has been painful for all of us over the years. Fortunately, the passage of time has partly helped to diminish the memory of that trauma.

We hired a car to drive to Heathrow Airport. Our scheduled flight to Los Angeles departed mid-morning. Our goodbyes were not easy, especially for the twins. We all hugged each other with tears in our eyes and said our goodbyes. As we drove slowly out of their driveway in south Birmingham, Judy and I glanced back to where Janet, Albert, and their two young boys were standing together by their front entrance, waving us goodbye. We waved our final farewell, our eyes streaming with tears.

I estimated the journey to Heathrow would take less than two hours. The trip to the airport was subdued and the tension between Judy and me was difficult to manage. We spoke very little to each other, as we were both upset. Fortunately, the children slept in the back seat of the car for most of the journey. I didn't regret the decision we had made and I knew that we had to keep a focus on what we were doing. I managed to stay positive, as the alternative view would not sustain us as a family unit. Leaving to live in another country was always going to be a difficult challenge, but I was convinced we would eventually succeed.

Our aircraft left on time and the Air New Zealand DC8 began its lengthy polar flight towards Los Angeles. The twelve-hour flying time gave Judy and me the time to reflect. Our children were excited as this was their first long haul flight and their upbeat demeanour strengthened our resolve to succeed.

We spent two nights in Los Angeles and on the second morning caught a taxi to the airport. Our intention was to spend the day in Anaheim, to visit Disney World before returning to catch the evening flight to Auckland. Before boarding the bus to Anaheim, we placed our suitcases for safekeeping in the left-luggage lockers in the terminal building. The journey took just over eighty minutes and the bus dropped us off at the Disneyland Hotel.

Outside the hotel car park was a high monorail system, leading into the amusement park. As the shiny train entered the complex, ahead of us was a silhouette cast against the blue Californian skyline; a magical fairy castle and the white slopes of the Matterhorn. The public-address system on the train continually informed us of the wonders of the magical kingdom, from exotic jungles, to fairy-tale princesses and *Pirates of the Caribbean,* to underwater submarine voyages. They all triggered our children's imagination. Nicola and Matthew were overjoyed. Our only conundrum was how we were going to visit all the attractions in one day.

Nicola wanted to take a ride, climbing a scale model of the Matterhorn, so I left Matthew with Judy, who decided to introduce our son to the delights of American soft ice cream. By the end of the afternoon, we had experienced many, but not all of the rides within the theme park. Nicola's favourite was the Haunted House. This required participants to stand inside a large room, furnished as a library. Suddenly the lights dimmed and the floor descended as the walls around us appeared to simultaneously slide downwards. To complete the experience, the ceiling began to descend towards us, giving the feeling it was going to crash down on our heads. It was of course an illusion, but the sense of excitement it generated, only made us want to experience more attractions within the magical kingdom.

Matthew's favourite, was *Alice in Wonderland,* which involved participants boarding an oversized caterpillar, painted in bright yellow and brown stripes. It was only just large enough for two adults and two children. We all sat back as the caterpillar moved around an open-air arena, depicting themes from Lewis Carroll's epic novel. We met and engaged with different characters, Tweedle Dee and Tweedle Dum, The Mad Hatter, The Queen of Hearts, The Cheshire Cat and of course, Alice herself.

The day's adventure in Anaheim gave us a chance to spend a family day in the Californian sunshine, just having fun. It provided a respite from the sadness of leaving our families and friends in England. When we eventually left the park and caught our bus back to the airport, we were all tired and exhausted from a fabulous day out. Our first task after arriving at the terminal was to retrieve our suitcases. We had hired two lockers and after retrieving two large cases, I open the door of the second locker. It was completely empty.

We found out later that other people had experienced a similar outcome. The setup was all too familiar. Criminal elements would scout the area around the baggage halls and look for travellers, who like us, were taking a day trip away from the airport. This negative incident left us feeling very low. We had travel insurance, but many of the items stolen were of a sentimental nature and irreplaceable. All our special photographs of the family, Matthew's raggedy Rupert Bear, and Nicola's cherished comfort blanket were gone forever.

After checking in for our flight, we were all looking forward to a few hours of sleep. Our fifteen-hour flight to New Zealand had a short fuel stop in Honolulu before the final leg to Auckland. The children slept well during most of the flight, but Judy and I tossed and turned. I kept thinking of Mum and Dad and how they attempted to put on a brave face on our departure. When we left their house, we all recognised the pain they really felt inside. We had all failed to express any real emotion, in case we upset each other – our tears were deferred for later on.

As I sat in my window seat, I reflected on saying goodbye to Monica and her husband Brian. We had said our farewells to them a week earlier, but the process lacked any emotion or real regret from either side. The emotional gap between us, established over so many years, was such that even our parting failed to prompt some meaningful exchange or bonhomie between us.

Two hours before we arrived in Auckland, all passengers received a certificate from the cabin crew. Purportedly signed by the captain, the certificate provided evidence for each passenger flying over the International Date Line. Our new life was about to begin.

Chapter 8

By June 1980, Six years of our lives had gone by. Nicola would shortly be twelve and Matthew would be nine. I was driving home from work, having left the office early in the afternoon. Judy and the children were visiting England, spending the summer with her mother and twin sister, I was feeling desperately alone and abandoned. The heavy winter rain was beating down on my windscreen and I turned the switch to increase the wiper speed on full. I was finding it increasingly difficult to see clearly through the glass in front of me. Reducing speed quickly, I left the main road and turned in to a nearby side street.

As I applied the brake and stopped, the rain began to disperse. I could hardly see a thing; tears were streaming down the side of my face and I was shaking uncontrollably. 'Pull yourself together,' I said to myself, echoing what Dad would have said if he had been there.

I waited in the car for a few more minutes before regaining my composure and then continued to drive back slowly to our cold empty house in the northern suburbs. The week before, I had written to Mum and Dad, telling them how much I missed Judy and the children. It was a short letter and failed to express any real emotion. More importantly it failed to say how I had really been feeling since their recent visit to Auckland over Christmas 1979 and the early few months of summer 1980. Their holiday

Down Under had been a special time for all of us. It gave us all a chance to reconnect, especially for our children.

When they left Auckland to return to England, Judy and I drove them to the airport. Both of them had really enjoyed the contrast of visiting a very different culture, to what they were used to in England. Mum enjoyed the freedom of walking to the beach for an early morning swim and Dad often remarked how, if he had been a younger man, how he could have built a new life in New Zealand.

After the children had fare-welled their grandparents at our home, we left them both with friends. At the airport, I felt so sad as Mum and Dad proceeded to the departure gate. I walked back towards Mum just before she passed out of sight and gave her a long special hug. Dad turned towards me saying, 'Let's not get too emotional.' I turned away smiling, while continuing to wave back as they walked through the departure gate. Deep down inside, I cried my heart out.

Ever since we had arrived in Auckland, the unresolved issue of my adoption constantly crossed my mind. I never faced the issue head-on; I just suppressed the desire, pushing the question to the back of my mind. Building a new life in New Zealand required a strong commitment from Judy and myself, in particular during those early years. Having decided to stay in New Zealand, although there were occasions when we seriously considered going back to England, we stayed, because new opportunities kept arising which we continued to successfully exploit. More pertinently, it was because the children had settled quickly and were happy.

Winter in Auckland is notoriously damp. That evening before preparing my evening meal, I lit the cast-iron potbelly. The living room quickly began to feel warm and homely and my mood improved. I felt emotionally drained by the experience in the car that afternoon and began to reflect on what was happening and where I was heading.

Life had been good to us since our arrival in Auckland back in 1974. I had a good job, the children were doing well at school and Judy had taken up show jumping, fulfilling an earlier ambition to work with horses. I had nothing to complain about, yet over the preceding months I was experiencing waves of depression and not knowing how to deal with it.

In hindsight there were two key issues; firstly Dad and I had failed to express our feelings to each other. Secondly my need to talk openly about my adoption had been suppressed by the guilt I carried deep inside me. I needed some help. The next morning I decided to engage in cognitive therapy and I began a series of appointments with a psychologist to explore my concerns.

A few weeks later, I wrote a long letter to Dad. I told him how I really felt. It was a difficult letter for me to compose and as I proceeded on this journey of discovery I meticulously retained copies of all the correspondence. My letter read as follows:

Dear Dad,

I write to you today because I have had a bit of a breakdown. This letter is about me and I want to say a lot to you and Mum. When you left Auckland I felt so sad. When we all said goodbye at the gate, I held Mum closely and you said, "Let's not get too emotional" and I cried inside.

My parents were leaving me, the only people I had ever known as parents who love me and I wanted to be very outgoing towards both of you. It brought to my mind a letter you wrote to me on my 21st birthday, wishing me love and happiness for the future. In one paragraph you mentioned that you hoped the future would bring me much sunshine, with little shadow.

Today is a day that the shadow is here and I especially need your love and understanding. There have been many times over the years that we have tried to move towards really understanding each other. I turn back again to your letter where you said, "I still sometimes nag, but it should be interpreted as a form of self-defence due to my inability to really help." Your potential for caring is so immense, yet as you said, your inability to really help and show your feelings is a loss to us both.

When I have brought up on various occasions the subject of my adoption, I know you have tried to be frank with me from the earliest times. I must admit that deep down inside me, I have felt guilty in asking you for more details. It is only today that I have taken the courage to face up to the situation.

I don't care what the circumstances of my birth parents were; whether sad, happy or bad. As I write this letter, I cry that I have had to ask you like this.

I have always tried to follow your example by showing a stiff upper lip, although I have not always succeeded. I want to know who I am and where I came from. Please understand that my love for you both is as strong as ever and under my skin I just wish to share deep emotions with you both. You have both brought me up and have given me everything. No one can ever take that away.

Please bear with me, in what is a difficult and painful time for me and write to me soon. I am presently working with a clinical psychologist, who is a great help. When we next meet, please allow me to express the love that I have for you, in a way that I want to express it.

All my love, Paul[24]

---

[24] Paul G. Denny to Charles G. Denny, June 25, 1980.

***

I posted the letter and a few weeks later I received a reply.

Dear Paul,

Your letter has us desperately worried, we feel so far away and overwhelmed with a feeling that we have somehow let you down. I particularly seem to have quite unwittingly shut you out and that is completely contrary to my deepest feelings.

At Auckland Airport, when the sadness of parting was hitting us all and tears were in our hearts if not in our eyes, I foolishly tried to lighten the tension by jocularly suggesting we should avoid getting too emotional and thus intruded into your deeply appreciated fond hugging of Mum. Instead of easing the heart ache, perhaps I added to it. Please forgive the old fool, like the dear son you are.

I advisedly use that form of address, not for nothing, as nobody could make us think of you as other than our boy, our own dear son. Way back in the very early days, some doubtless, well-meaning idiot asked. 'But what if you have a child of your own later?' We replied, that would be grand – a brother or sister for our first son Paul.'

But though that is how we have always felt, we of course played no part in the first three months of your life. That you should want to know something of that time and your natural parents, particularly when battling through an emotional crisis, is quite understandable. But why feel distressed at seeking information or getting upset at approaching us for it. Where else could you seek it!

Please don't imagine that we feel hurt or slighted. Our Paul wants to know something of his origin. Such little

186

information as we have is his by right. It in no way affects the deep love and affection between us – adoptive mums and dads and sons and daughters.

Unfortunately, we have not got many details. You came into our life through the good offices of the Northamptonshire R.C. Child Welfare and Adoption Society. I have to rely upon memory, for the only document we retained is a copy of your adoption certificate. From memory you were born at St. Joseph's Home in Grayshott and your mother was an Irish girl in service, surname McBride. Your father was a serving soldier and your name was Michael McBride before adoption. That, Paul, is the sum total of the information we received.

You suggest reluctance and even a feeling of guilt in asking me for such details. In pity's name why old son? Perhaps we should have volunteered the information and thus saved you the embarrassment of asking for it. Forgive our insensitivity; it all seemed very past history. As we did in 1946, we still thank God that young McBride became Paul Gerard Denny, who has brought so much happiness (oh yes and a few anxieties, motor cycles etc, etc, etc.) to Mum and me and so splendidly perpetuated the name of Denny in his own delightful family.

I really did appreciate our times together on the last trip to Auckland. I had commented to Mum that we seemed to have drawn much closer, yet perhaps if I had been more outgoing, a little less hidebound – stiff upper-lipped, or pompous – take your pick, we should have openly acknowledged the deep bond of love that links us, although we are on opposite sides of the world.

In retrospect, it is easy to appreciate how inadequately one can express oneself. While I have often said, we cannot live our children's lives for them; it could perhaps seem to display disinterest. That is so far from the truth. Your happiness and prosperity are desperately important to us and are always in the forefront of our prayers. However,

187

we must not presume to dictate or impose our selfish plans upon you. We can only hope and pray that any advice we proffer may keep you to the decision that will ultimately bring you happiness and true fulfilment. If in so doing, we have ever given the impression that your plans were nothing to do with us, except to endorse them, then we have indeed given a false impression. That your best prospects for a full, successful life have taken you and Judy and our grandchildren so far distant from us in miles, is a grief to us, but you remain very close in our thoughts and hearts.

So in closing, let me reiterate those sentiments expressed from our love for you in December 1967 and felt so earnestly today. May the future bring you much happiness and sunshine with very little shadow.[25]

Fondest love to you all from us both – As ever

Dad

I replied to Dad's letter at the end of July, the week before Judy and the children returned from England. Dad's letter had meant so much to me; it was the first time I had experienced that degree of intimacy and honesty about how we both felt towards each other. In my reply I expressed I was feeling much better. As well, I explained the decision I had made to leave paid employment and start my own business in partnership with a trusted business colleague. My immediate plans required extensive travel overseas, which would commence from the end of August. I ended the letter by telling them from the 4th of September I wanted to spend ten days with them in their retirement cottage located in the Cotswolds.

---

[25] Charles G. Denny to Paul G. Denny, July 4, 1980.

They received my letter within four days, which amazed us both and Dad replied upon receipt. They were thrilled that I was coming to stay with them and alluded to the opportunity of being able to engage "in a long natter."

I arrived in the Cotswold town of Fairford as planned. My prime purpose was to build on the sentiment expressed in our exchange of letter, as well as relax and enjoy being at home again. Dad was getting on in age and would be seventy-one in December, while Mum was sixty-eight. On most days, I drove them to a favourite pub where we enjoyed lunch together, combined with a pint of our favourite beer for the men and a glass of wine for Mum. We never broached the subject of adoption again. I don't know why, maybe we didn't need too, as there was no more they could tell me about my origins. In 1980 the legal position in England prevented public access to adoption records. The only exception was with a Court order. It would have been unlikely I would be able to obtain any further information through legal channels. I just accepted the door was closed to progress and the situation was *fait accompli*.

My new business prospered throughout the rest of the decade. This allowed me the time and finances to indulge in many visits to England. I always spent around two weeks with Mum and Dad annually and as the years went by both my parent's health gradually declined.

***

During those ten years, my main focus of attention was the business. I was in my prime and both my business partner and I had set a clear objective when commencing the business back in September 1980. It was our intention to build a profitable freight forwarding, warehousing and customs brokerage business and eventually sell the enterprise as a going concern. The process took the decade to achieve. We were successful in our planned endeavour and sold the business to a large German multi-national. As part of that agreement, I resigned from the company at the end of December 1990.

Before leaving, I had spent many weeks considering what I would do with my life. I had the opportunity of having time on my side, having entered into a restraint of trade agreement with the new proprietors. This meant I was unable to work in the same industry for a minimum of three years. My business partner decided to stay with the organisation, working with the new owners. I made the decision to spend a month with Mum and Dad and think about my next career move. Fortuitously the respite gave me time and freedom to revisit the question of my adoption.

I arrived in England a few days after the 1991 New Year celebrations. My flight arrived at Heathrow before dawn and I picked up my hire car and drove to the Cotswolds. It was bitterly cold and the roads had patches of black ice to test an Antipodean's driving skills. I reached their cottage just after eight in the morning. Dad was in his eighty-second year and in poor health and Mum would celebrate her seventy-ninth birthday in March. Looking after Dad was taking its strain on Mum's health and I hadn't seen either of them for a couple of years. Time and ageing had really taken their toll and I was shocked at how the last two years had reduced their quality of life.

On my previous visit to their picturesque stone cottage we would go out in my car and drive in the beautiful Cotswold countryside. This visit precluded travelling by car due to Dad's ill health. Instead, I tried to assist Mum with the many tasks she endured, accentuated by Dad's incapacity. Some days Mum and I would leave Dad for a few hours sitting in his fireside chair. We would go out together for lunch, after having shopped for supplies in a nearby country town. Mum and I appreciated the special time we had together, but our enjoyment was lessened by our concern for Dad.

I had a lot of time on my hands with time to reflect. I took the opportunity of walking daily for two or three hours in the local countryside. As I contemplated my future plans, I also began to think more about my adoption. I wanted to share the ideas churning though my mind, but Mum and Dad were preoccupied with their own concerns. It just didn't feel like the right time to share my thoughts. For them, their main priority was health issues. Their physical decline and distress caused by ill health would not be mitigated by telling them what I intended to do. Paradoxically, as they became frail, it became easier for me to make up my mind. I decided to begin looking for information on my adoption.

The suppressed yearning I felt to search for my birth mother can be explained in research conducted in Canada during 1995, where one adoptee described the motivation for his search as: "… a need for biological connection. I felt a vacuum there, because I was unrelated to people. I didn't have any ties or connections to anyone in this world other than myself. My adoptive parents, even my wife and children. It's different somehow. I wanted an anchor, to connect me. Make me real".[26]

The solitude of the daily walks gave me the chance to formulate a strategy. The idea of a plan became compelling. I decided to compile a journal to document my forthcoming search, in case I lost my way. It felt like walking over slippery stones in a rushing stream. I had no idea what the outcome of my search would provide; to feel safe and

---

[26] Karen March. "Perception of Adoption as Social Stigma: Motivation for Search and Reunion." *Journal of Marriage and Family* 57, no. 3 (1995): p. 657.

secure in the journey, I needed to retain a physical record of my actions.

My journey commenced from the following premise. I knew my original name and where I was born; St Joseph's Home, Grayshott, Hampshire. I figured my birth mother would have been a Catholic. She was Irish. I assumed she would have wanted her child adopted within a Catholic family. I also guessed that back in 1945, I would have been christened at the local Catholic Church.

The following week I told Mum and Dad I was going away for a couple of days on the pretext of visiting friends in London. I hated lying to them, but again I could see no advantage for them in knowing about my plans. I left by car for Hampshire, a journey of less than three hours. It was mid-winter and the weather was cold and wet. I had chosen to stay for the night in a small hotel in Hindhead a few miles from Grayshott.

Once I had checked into my room, I began to scour the telephone book for the address of the local Catholic Church and St Joseph's Home. My search for the church was rewarded and I scribbled down the address in my notebook. I wasn't so lucky with St Joseph's as no listing was given.

That evening I had dinner alone in the hotel restaurant and afterwards I spent the evening in the bar. Once I had ordered my first pint of ale, I asked the barman had he heard of St Joseph's Home.

'Sorry sir – never heard of the place.' The barman went away to serve another patron. After a few minutes, he returned to where I was standing at the bar.

'They may have changed the name,' he said, as he finished serving another customer. 'I've lived around these parts for many a year, I'll ask around and let you know.'

'Thanks,' I said. 'But I'm leaving tomorrow morning, so if you do hear anything I'd really appreciate it.'

'Will do,' he replied, casually.

I felt utterly dejected. I picked up my pint and looked away from the bar. I had naively assumed the children's home would still exist and after another beer, I decided to go to bed early. The barman had been well intentioned, but he never broached the topic again. My plan for tomorrow was to drive the short distance to St Joseph's Catholic Church and see what I could discover.

After breakfast, I checked out from the hotel. It was only a short distance to St Joseph's Church and I parked the car in front of the presbytery which adjoined the church.

Knocking on the front door, an elderly man wearing a black suit opened the door. I recognised his white dog collar and asked.

'Excuse me Father, my name is Paul Denny. I was born in Grayshott in 1945. I now live in New Zealand. I'm trying to find information concerning my adoption. Would you be able to help me?'

I could tell from his face that this wasn't the first time he had been asked a similar question. 'Come inside,' he said, with a friendly smile. Closing the door, he led me towards a small meeting room.

'That's a long time ago, how long are you staying in England?' he asked.

'Just for a month, Father, I fly back to Auckland in early February.'

When we reached the meeting room, we both sat at a small table.

'I always wanted to visit Australia and New Zealand. Paul, do you know what name you were given at birth?'

Inside I was beginning to feel a mixed sense of trepidation and anticipation. What new information would I find?

'My adoptive parents told me my original name was Michael McBride,' I said, almost bursting into tears. I could feel my heart racing inside me.

The priest looked empathetically across the table. 'Paul, what month were you born?'

'December the twelfth,' I said, quickly. 'I was born at St. Joseph's Home.'

I haven't heard of St Joseph's Home,' he said kindly, 'I think you may mean a place named *Assisi*, it's not far from the church. It's only half a mile away, down Hammer Lane, opposite the church.'

'My dad told me he thought the home was named St Joseph's – he must have got it wrong,' I said.

'Doesn't matter, it was a long time ago. I'm sure it's Assisi – that was the only home around these parts for girls giving up their babies for adoption. It's a large house and was converted into three private homes some years back,' he replied kindly.

Rising slowly from his chair, he moved across towards a tall dusty bookcase. The shelves were crammed. He brought back a large register with the words, *Baptisms 1937 – 1947,* imprinted on the volumes hardback spine.

The priest placed the closed ledger onto the table. As he began to thumb through the pages he said, 'The twelfth of December, didn't you say?' to which I nodded anxiously in reply.

'I'm afraid all the records are written in Latin,' he said, slowly turning the pages of handwritten script.

'I've got one name here – this sounds like it,' he continued, adjusting his glasses.

We both stared down at the page of the register. In the left-hand column was the date, the sixteenth of December 1945 and to the right was the name Richard Michael McBride. I couldn't read any more as tears welled up in my eyes. It was the first time I had connected directly with my full original name – it was a milestone in the process of understanding who I was.

'Sorry Father,' I said wiping my eyes. 'I didn't expect to react like this.'

'That's fine – don't get yourself upset. You won't be the first to have come here looking to find information about your past. Let me write out a copy of the record for you,' he said, picking up his pen.

The priest then prepared a copy of the Certificate of Baptism. The most important new information on the certificate was; I was the son of Bridget Enda McBride.

As we left the meeting room, the priest asked me would I like to visit the church next door. I followed him down a corridor leading to a side entrance into the church. As we entered the building, my eyes were drawn to the stone baptismal font. Seeing the place where I had been christened all those years ago brought all my emotions to the surface. The tears streamed down my face.

'It's been a big day for you Paul, why don't you drive down Hammer Lane and see the house where you were born?' he said, as I struggled to pull myself together.

'Yes, I will Father, and thank you for all your time and understanding.'

We walked from the church into the car park. The priest pointed across the road, confirmed the directions to Hammer Lane and shaking hands, we said goodbye.

'Thanks again Father,' I said as he turned and walked back towards the presbytery. The drive to *Assisi* was less than a mile. The house was a large Edwardian dwelling, easily visible from the road. I parked the car outside. I walked towards the entrance gate and knocked on the front door of the first dwelling. A friendly woman answered the door and I explained who I was and why I had come.

'We get many people knocking on the door telling us the same thing. Why don't you come into the grounds and look around. It will give you an excellent view of the house,' she said, with a welcoming smile.

'Thanks so much,' I said.

Before she went back into the house she asked, 'Would you like a drink of tea? I'll bring it out to the garden for you in a few minutes.'

'That would be great,' I replied, as I walked across to a large gate leading into the grounds.

The two storey red brick house had large gracious gardens sloping down towards extensive woodlands. Although the main building was subdivided, the grounds were shared. In the gardens were reminders of the legacy the house had once provided. The orphanage had previously been managed by Catholic nuns. In the well-ordered grounds were two religious statues, built around a stone grotto.

'How long have you lived here?' I asked, as the woman brought the tea out on a tray.

'It must be four years at least,' she replied. 'My husband and I retired to Grayshott. Our daughter lives close by.'

'It's a beautiful part of the country,' I said. 'Do you have grandchildren?'

'Yes two, a boy and a girl,' she replied.

I finished drinking my tea. Before she bade me goodbye, she gave some information on the local area and its history. I told her I was keen to trace my birth mother and she wished me good luck with the search.

'Thanks so much for letting me see the grounds,' I said.

'The best of luck with your search,' she said, walking back towards the house. 'I hope you find the information you want.'

I opened the gate and walked back to my car. It was important to have seen the house, although I did not see inside. Walking in the gardens of the house had provided a tranquil moment to reflect on what my next step would be. Now that I knew my original name, I decided the next step was to obtain a copy of my full birth certificate. I figured my birth would have been registered by the nuns. In Dad's letter he had mentioned, I had only been adopted three months after my birth.

I drove back towards the main road. After reaching the centre of Grayshott, I parked close to the local Post Office. Inside, I went up to the counter asking, 'Where was the nearest place to Grayshott where one could register a birth?'

The obliging clerk behind the desk gave a down-to-earth response. 'The nearest Register Office is in Petersfield – it's only a few miles away.'

Thanks,' I said, before leaving. 'You've been a great help.'

When I got back to the car, I felt flushed with excitement. I drove quickly towards Petersfield, overwhelmed with anticipation of what further information I would discover. I arrived after lunch and met with the woman registrar. She was very helpful. I explained who I was and that I wanted a copy of my original birth certificate. As I had mentioned that I was adopted on my arrival, the registrar made it very clear she was unable to issue the document unless I knew my birth mother's full name, my full name at birth, and the date and place of birth.

I now possessed all the information she required and it felt empowering. She was satisfied with my response and asked me to wait in her office.

'I will be back in a few minutes, after I've located the original records,' she said, leaving the room.

When she returned, she carried a large ledger under her arm.

'I would not have been able to give you this information if you hadn't disclosed the information you gave me earlier,' she said, looking directly towards me. 'You told me earlier you had been adopted. Because you possess this statutory information, any person can access it. Therefore I can see no justifiable legal reason why you should not obtain a copy of the birth certificate.'

She placed the ledger on the desk between us. After thumbing through the pages from the 12th of December 1945, she soon reached the correct entry. The registrar wrote out a certified copy of the birth certificate. Passing the document to me the first piece of new information was my mother's address and occupation; domestic cook, Wootton House, Aylesbury, Buckinghamshire.

I left Petersfield, having thanked the registrar and decided to head for Fairford. I had promised Mum and Dad I would only be away for a couple of days. They had invited Monica and her husband and their two young children to lunch on the coming Sunday and I hadn't seen them for a couple of years. As I drove back from Hampshire, I realised I needed to absorb and think about the information I had obtained and what my next step needed to be.

If my birth mother had worked as a cook, it was obvious that forty-seven years later; she was unlikely to be still working there. My mind began to race with a cocktail of scenarios all of which made no sense. She may have moved and was still living in the area, or had moved away from the district. I concluded that I needed to research Wootton House. The closest town was Aylesbury and the best place to start was likely to be the public library. I decided to spend the Monday in Aylesbury, following Monica's visit and try to find out more.

When I arrived back at Mum and Dad's house, they were anxious to hear more about my two day trip away. I detected from the tone of their voices that my story of going to see a friend in London had been less than convincing. I stuck to my original narrative. Dad didn't try to push me into giving further details of my few days away, but his tone of voice made it clear he wasn't satisfied with my explanation.

'I don't think we will ever really find out where you've been,' he said, looking towards Mum with an expression of resignation. Whether they guessed what my intentions were, I will never know; the subject never came up again. Riddled with guilt, I just couldn't tell them the truth. I thought it would hurt them. That was the way we dealt with difficult subjects; pushed the matter under the carpet, or told a white lie, hoping it would all just go away.

At noon on Sunday, Monica, her husband Brian and their two children arrived for lunch. They lived an hour's drive away, in a small town close to The Forest of Dean. Shortly after their arrival, Brian and I decided to walk to the centre of Fairford and sink a couple of pints of ale. It gave us a chance to catch up. Dad had been depressed again and combined with his other ailment, was proving difficult to manage. Monica was her usual self and gave the impression she would rather have been somewhere else. Brian mentioned, as we were drinking our second pint, that Monica had been depressed over recent times.

When we got back to the house, lunch was almost ready. The combined lounge and dining room was sufficient space for Mum and Dad. When friends or family arrived, space was at a premium. Dad had his meal on a tray, while sitting in his armchair. The four adults sat around the gate leg table by the window, and the two children ate their lunch within earshot on stools in the adjacent kitchen. The conversation among the seated adults was sadly less than engaging. The meal finished with a choice of biscuits and cheese, with ice-cream for the children. Brian and I helped clear the dishes and we both did the washing up in the confines of the tiny kitchen. After we had finished and poured Monica and the children their second glass of cola, we prepared well-earned cups of tea for Mum and Dad.

By two o'clock, Monica announced they all needed to travel back home. The excuse was she had preparation work to complete for school the following day. Monica worked as a primary teacher and education was her passion. As they all left the house, Mum and I waved goodbye at the front door, while Dad chose to remain in his chair, having previously bade his farewell. I had attempted to engage with Monica, but again was unsuccessful. With Brian and the children I had no such problem. Once again we all covertly accepted that when Monica and I were in the same space, the dialogue between us was either strained, or noticeably absent.

On Monday morning I rose early and drove to Aylesbury. I had told Mum and Dad I was out with friends for the day and they fortunately seemed to accept the explanation. I arrived at the library by midmorning and started my research. The staff was very helpful and directed me to a range of material. I wasn't really sure what to look for, but decided to research the house where my birth mother had worked all those years ago.

Wotton House was built between 1704 and 1714 and is an excellent example of English Baroque architecture.[27] The house lies in the small Buckinghamshire village of Wotton Underwood, a few miles to the West of Aylesbury and was the home of the Grenville family. In 1820 the

[27] Wikipedia contributors, "Wotton House," *Wikipedia, The Free Encyclopedia,*
http://en.wikipedia.org/w/index.php?title=Wotton_House&oldid=600595718 (accessed July 1, 2014).

interior of the building was destroyed by fire and the owner, the 2nd Marquess of Buckingham restored the building.[28] The house was inherited by a succession of Grenvilles until 1889, and rented to various tenants.[29] In 1929 the property and the surrounding estate was purchased by the MP for Aylesbury, Major Michael Beaumont.[30] The Beaumont family eventually vacated the property in 1947 and the property fell into disrepair and became derelict.

By 1957 the property was scheduled for demolition by Buckinghamshire County Council and two weeks prior, the main house and the Clock Pavilion were purchased for six thousand pounds paid in six annual payments.[31] The new owners, Mrs Elaine Brunner and her husband, moved into Wotton House and began the task of restoring the building to its former glory. Her husband died in 1966 and she spent the rest of her life dedicated to the restoration project.[32]

As the story of Wotton House unfolded before my eyes, the last piece of information I retrieved, confirmed Elaine Brunner still lived in the house. It seemed elementary to me; the most obvious thing to do was to make contact by telephone. Once I had left the library, I looked out for a public telephone box, scanned the directory and dialled Mrs Brunner's number.

---

[28] Wikipedia contributors, "Wotton House," *Wikipedia, The Free Encyclopedia*,
http://en.wikipedia.org/w/index.php?title=Wotton_House&oldid=600595718 (accessed July 1, 2014).

[29] ibid.

[30] ibid.

[31] Wotton House, The Independent,
http://www.independent.co.uk/news/obituaries/obituary-elaine-brunner-1155459.html (accessed July 1, 2014).

[32] ibid.

I apologised for calling and quickly explained I was looking for my birth mother who had lived at Wotton House in 1946. I quickly gathered from the tone of her reply that she was elderly and had difficulty in hearing. She was very gracious listening to my story, but had not heard of a woman named Enda McBride living in the vicinity. She suggested my mother may have married and as a consequence, her name would have changed. Being a typical male, combined with the emotional anticipation from the events of the last few days, something so obvious never occurred to me.

Before I put down the telephone, Elaine Brunner suggested I contact an agency in England, which assists families attempting to trace their relatives. Having thanked her for her empathy, she asked me to contact her again by letter and give her any new information I might obtain which may prompt her memory. As I walked back to my car, I impulsively decided to drive to Wotton Underwood and look around.

The journey from Aylesbury to Wotton Underwood is less than eight miles and the small quiet hamlet has an ancient church a few minutes' walk from Wotton House. A few scattered cottages blend into the landscape and the road access to the village terminates by the church. I decided to enter the church and soak up the atmosphere, before viewing the exterior of Wotton House.

Originally constructed between 1070 and 1130, stone remnants of the period are still visible. The church was extensively altered during the 15th and 19th centuries and many historians visit the Grenville Aisle within the church, which houses multiple stone coffins, built as chests of drawers. Buried within them, are the remains of generations of Grenvilles including three British Prime Ministers and three Dukes.[33]

As I left the church, I walked back to the road via the ancient churchyard. Closing the small five-bar wooden gate, I looked up towards the tree line and saw Wotton House. Set behind tall elms and standing in splendid parkland, the main house and its two pavilions are set back from the narrow road. The exterior of the principal house is constructed of red-brick, with nine distinctive rectangular brick chimneys rising from a weathered green copper roof.[34] The sash windows comprise thin glazed bars, furnished with stone architrave surrounds. I began to reflect on where my mother might have lived, as my eyes traced along the reflective glass windows. She must have often looked out on to the rolling countryside and now it was my turn to enjoy the view of the house and reflect on the memories she must have had. I just hoped my search for her would be eventually fulfilled.

The journey back to Fairford was preoccupied by thoughts provoked by my visit to Wotton Underwood. Racing through my mind were many questions; had my mother married? Did she still live locally? Did she have other children, and was she even alive? In particular, the first thing I needed to do when I returned to Auckland was to implement Elaine Brunner's advice. I needed to contact an agency which could investigate further, using the information I had already obtained.

I arrived back with Mum and Dad just after sunset. The first question they asked was predictable; how was your

---

33 The Bernwode Benefice, All Saints Church, Wotton. http://www.bernwodebenefice.com/wotton (accessed July 3, 2014).

34 British Listed Buildings, Wotton House, Wotton Underwood. http://www.britishlistedbuildings.co.uk/en-42550-wotton-house-with-walls-to-pavilions-wott (accessed July 3, 2014)

day? I felt guilty again, not being able to tell them the truth and where I had been and what I had learned. Dad looked depressed and Mum carried the burden as always, with dignified resignation. Before I could ask them how things were going Mum asked, 'Have you eaten, Paul?'

'I had a pub lunch Mum,' which was true, 'so I'm not that hungry. I might go out later this evening for a couple of pints – don't worry about me,' I replied with a reassuring smile. Then I went quickly upstairs to change, hoping the atmosphere would improve.

Mum and Dad were watching television when I returned to the living room. Both were now hard of hearing and the speakers on the television must have been working overtime. Dad was sitting in his armchair leaning forward towards the television. 'It will be cold tonight, Paul,' he said, not taking his eyes off the screen. 'There'll be black ice on the roads, so if you're driving, take extra care. Which pub will you be going to?'

'I might go to the Keepers Arms; I like it there and I can always get something to eat if I'm feeling hungry.'

'We haven't been back to the Keepers since your last visit,' said Mum regretfully. 'Dad and I often used to go there for lunch; it was one of our favourite pubs.'

I would have loved to take her to the Keepers for a drink. Mum would have politely refused if I had asked, as Dad would have been unable to go. That's what made our relationship so difficult; all of us were unable to really interact as we would have wished, burdened by either guilt or physical infirmity.

When I returned from the pub, the lights inside the house were out. Outside, a lofty street lamp filtered soft yellow light through the small front windows. My bedroom was on the third floor, accessed via two flights of narrow creaking stairs. I climbed the first flight, negotiated the short landing, passing quietly by my parents' bedroom.

Once passed their door, the old floorboards gave up their silence. As I reached the second flight, Mum's voice quietly asked.

'Paul – have you locked the front door?'

'Yes Mum, see you both tomorrow, sleep well,' I said, continuing up the last flight of stairs.

My bedroom was immediately above theirs. As I got into bed, the creaks from the old timbers ceased. The house was quiet and all I could see was the moonlight shining through the closed curtains of my dormer window. Swirling through my mind were the events of the day, but within a few minutes I fell into a deep sleep.

***

The last few days were difficult. I'd promised Mum I would take Dad to the doctor for his weekly check-up. Regrettably, I was unable to mitigate their decline in health, I felt so helpless. It took Dad ages to get dressed and ready for his appointment. I parked the car outside the cottage to try and make things easier. Parking restrictions prohibited leaving the car parked outside the house for long.

When Dad travelled, he always required his wheelchair. Once he was seated comfortably in the car, I packed the red and grey wheelchair in the boot. Mum and I got in and we drove to the surgery. Inside the car it was chilly, and outside, the winter wind was blowing bitterly cold. Even though Mum and Dad were well wrapped up, they were both feeling miserable.

We returned home following Dad's brief consultation, well-armed with repeat prescriptions for the multitude of ailments he endured. Mum entered the house while I unloaded the wheelchair. Once I had parked the car I returned to the house.

Dad was seated back in his fireside armchair. Mum was in the kitchen, making another pot of tea. 'Do you want a cup of tea, Paul?' Mum asked.

'No thanks, I fancy a walk down to the town. I can call in at the chemist and get Dad's prescription dispensed.'

'Thanks, Paul,' she said. 'I expect you'll go to The Bull's Head for a drink as well.'

'Sounds a good idea Mum – only for a quick pint though. I'll be back soon.'

As I left the house, Dad was asleep in his chair. I closed the heavy front door after saying goodbye to Mum and walked the short distance towards the town square. After leaving the chemist, I walked directly across the square and entered The Bull's Head. Mum would be preparing lunch, as this was their main meal of the day. I was mindful of my promise; I would only be away for a short while.

The welcoming lounge bar was unoccupied, yet warm, typical for a Monday morning. I stood at the bar after ordering my first pint. Shortly, a few local patrons entered the bar. Striking up a conversation, I chatted to one who I recognised; he was more acquaintance than friend. The conversation ranged from weekend sport results, to local gossip, and predictably concluded with speculation on prospects for the weather for the rest of the week. I left, feeling content after my second beer, walking back briskly and looking forward to lunch.

Mum had prepared a light meal of smoked salmon; set on a tray for Dad and at the table by the French window for us. The window looked out on to their small rear garden. A grey concrete path led down towards a dry-stone wall at the rear. The only plants were roses, which neighbours had kindly pruned back in the autumn. To the right of the pathway was a small cedar garden shed and close to the window, was a stone bird-bath.

Dad instructed, 'Be a good lad. Fetch Mum and yourself a glass of wine.'

'Don't you want a glass as well?' I asked.

'Not for me thanks, but you can fetch me a glass of cold water if you wouldn't mind?' he said, looking down towards his tray, continuing to eat his meal.

I left the table, returning with the two full glasses of Chardonnay from the open bottle in the refrigerator. I then went back and poured Dad a glass of chilled water. After placing the glass on his tray, he nodded in appreciation and I returned to my seat at the table.

As I started to eat, Mum was gazing out of the window. 'You'll be leaving us on Wednesday, after breakfast I expect. Just like last time?'

'Nice salmon, Mum,' I said, attempting to change the subject.

'Couldn't you stay for just a few more days,' she asked.

'I'd love to Mum, but I've got to get back and look for a new job. Judy and the children will be missing me.'

'I know,' she said. 'I do hope you'll come and see us again soon!'

'Of course I will Mum,' I said, trying to sound as optimistic as I could. Each time we parted we pretended I was not leaving, so I reminded them gently again.

'Mum – my flight leaves at two, so I'd like to get away early tomorrow morning.'

Neither of them responded immediately to my comment. I knew they were both regretting my forthcoming departure. Dad looked up, displaying his predictably melancholy face. Each time I left their cottage he always made the same remark.

'It may be the last time we will see you. Mum and I are not getting any younger.'

I always attempted to change the subject when he spoke like that. The euphemism was clear enough. Neither of us wanted to accept the reality of their own mortality.

By the time Wednesday morning arrived, all of us were putting on a brave face regarding my departure. The last two days in Fairford we had been spent chatting generally about Judy and the children and what my plans were when I returned to Auckland. Dad remarked it was a pity Monica had only been able to meet briefly when she came over for lunch and that on my next visit, we must spend more time together. I wasn't sure whether he meant with Monica or with them, but I guessed he was trying to put a positive spin on family reunions.

'Have another cup of tea before you go?' Mum asked, as I finished my third slice of buttered toast, covered with thick home-made marmalade.

'I'm fine Mum – I'll get plenty to eat and drink on the plane.' When I'd finished, I left the table and went upstairs for my heavy suitcase. After I had packed, I hauled the heavy case to the bottom of the stairs where Mum was waiting.

'Have you got everything?' she asked, as we both turned towards Dad, who was sitting in his chair.

'Think so Mum,' I said, leaning down, giving Dad a big hug.

'Take care – Look after yourself Laddie,' he said, catching my eye with his penetrating grey eyes. He then clasped my hand tightly. 'Give our love to Judy and the children. Let us know that you've arrived safely after you get back?'

'I will Dad – promise,' I said, turning towards Mum. I gave her a big hug and moved my suitcase towards the door. Opening the front door, I gave her a final embrace. 'Thanks for everything, Mum.'

I began walking towards my car, turning my head every few steps. Looking back, Mum was still waving at the door. I drove slowly past as she stood alone at the door. We continued to wave to each other until I turned at the ancient stone bridge spanning the River Colne. She was almost out of view. The eclipse of her frail silhouette in my rear-view mirror waving fondly was my final memory of that visit to Fairford.

Chapter 9

I arrived back home in Auckland in February 1991. The New Zealand summer was a welcome change from the bleak English winter. Judy met me at the airport and as we drove home, we chatted about the children and what plans I had regarding future employment. Nicola and Matthew were now working fulltime, although they both still lived at home.

As we settled back together into our New Zealand lifestyle, the seasonal hot, humid weather favoured alfresco dining. During the summer months, most evening meals were eaten in the garden, where our terracotta terrace provided a perfect venue to enjoy outdoor living. Most weekends, friends would join us for dinner and we took advantage of the warm lazy evenings to enjoy a glass or two of wine.

Our house overlooked the sea and Matthew took advantage of the ocean as a member of the local sailing club. Nicola was soon to start a nursing career, beginning her studies later that year. Judy spent much of her leisure time attending to her horse, as she was now an avid equestrian, competing regularly in dressage events.

I was happy to be back in Auckland. Although I missed England and the special time I had with Mum and Dad, the focus was now on our future. Judy was very encouraging about what I had learned in England concerning my adoption. Without her continual encouragement to pursue my quest, I doubt I would have had the courage and tenacity to continue with the search.

Both our children were also very supportive and encouraged me to continue with my investigation, particularly because they understood why the issue was so important to me. From their perspective they already had grandparents from Judy's side, as well as Mum and Dad, whom they accepted as their own kith and kin. Although they felt protective towards their grandparents whom they already knew and loved, they never perceived my inquiry as a challenge to that kinship. I am eternally grateful to them both for their love and understanding. At that stage in their lives my inquiry could have been a diversion for them.

A few days after my return home, the telephone rang. It was a beautiful Monday morning and it would have been around ten o'clock. Judy was out feeding her horse. I picked up the receiver in our bedroom and answered with a spring in my step.

'Hello, Paul speaking.'

'It's Mum here, I have some terrible news.' The tone in her voice sounded distressed. 'It's about Monica.'

I responded with the obvious question, 'What's happened?' she replied.

'Monica's dead. Brian found her in bed, after returning from an early Sunday morning walk.'

The air inside my lungs felt completely sucked out. I couldn't think or speak clearly. I slumped down on the side of the bed staring blankly at the floor.

'Mum, can I phone you back.' I said, I was hardly able to hear my own voice. 'I can't talk properly, I'm so sorry.'

'Call me back in an hour dear. It must be a terrible shock, especially being so far from home.'

'Mum, I'll call back as soon as I can.' I said, replacing the receiver on its cradle. Placing my open hands against my face, I cried my eyes out. In the back of my mind, I always feared something like this would happen. My first feeling was of absolute sadness and dismay, for her, her husband Brian and their two children. Mum had not mentioned the cause of death, but her words; 'found her in bed' indicated Monica may have ended her own life.

I phoned back an hour later. It was Sunday night, her time. Mum answered.

'Hello Mum – I am so sad. What happened? Where did we all go wrong?'

I waited in silence for her to reply. After a brief pause, tearfully, we began to exchange a few words.

'Brian found her when he returned from his morning walk. The two children were asleep in bed. He called the police straight way.'

'How's Brian coping?' I asked.

'He's been so supportive to us both, even with the burden of his own grief.'

'How's Dad, I asked.

'Just devastated – we both are. We feel we somehow let her down.'

'It's not your fault, Mum. We all tried to understand Monica. Somehow, we never did enough. I'm so sorry.'

The language we used expressed the deep guilt we felt. Why hadn't we recognised Monica's distress and why hadn't we been able to prevent such a dreadful tragedy from happening.

'There was nothing you could have done Paul. We only wish Dad and I had been able to do more,' she said slowly, in a tone of deep sadness.

We spoke for a few more minutes. All of us needed time to reflect on the terrible nature of what had happened. Before I said goodbye, I asked to speak to Dad.

'Dad sends his love, he's just too distraught to talk at the moment.

'Give Dad my love, Mum.'

Before the call ended, we agreed to write to each other. Somehow being able to write about our feelings would be easier. We expressed our love for each other and said goodbye. I walked into the lounge, sat down and faced the solitude alone.

Monica had died a few days before her forty-third birthday. Later in the day I took out a pen and began to draft a letter to Mum and Dad. Expressing my feelings of sorrow on paper helped me gather my thoughts. The central theme was the regret I felt at not having succeeded in establishing a meaningful connection with Monica. That sense of absolute guilt was echoed in their separate correspondence in reply to my letter.

Dear Paul,

Thank you for your nice and understanding letter. I'm afraid none of us ever really understood Monica's complex nature – maybe we as parents failed somewhere. I don't know, and we never shall. There was no note and no explanation of any kind. She is now at peace, which is what she must have sought and we can only continue to pray for her soul...

Fond love to Judy & the family & of course to you.
Mum xxx[35]

---

[35] Dora N. Denny to Paul G. Denny, February 23, 1991.

Dear Paul,

Mum has expressed our thanks for your much appreciated letter, but again thank you. It is so difficult to find words appropriate at a time like this, but be sure you have nothing to reproach yourself about, we all have misgivings and regrets over past omissions, but there is nothing we can do, except pray. Mum has been splendid over the past two weeks, despite her grief. She is the strength of our family and I am sure that Brian has been supported and comforted by her love. I shall always remember how her face crumpled when he broke the news to her over the phone and how she rallied almost immediately...

As ever, Dad xxx[36]

The sentiments they both expressed in their letters reflected a deep sense of hurt and failure as parents. Words were not sufficient to express the regret and pain they endured. Their coping mechanism was, as usual, to suppress their inner feelings.

Following Monica's death, eventually the passage of time helped the family to come to terms with their loss. Mum and Dad never referred to Monica's passing in any of their future communications, either by letter or telephone. Their health continued to decline as the year progressed and Judy and I made the decision we would endeavour to have time off in England the following year, principally to visit Mum and Dad.

***

---

[36] Charles G. Denny to Paul G. Denny, February 23, 1991.

Autumn begins officially in New Zealand in March and by then I had secured employment. I had delayed writing to Elaine Brunner at Wotton House as I had promised during my visit the previous year. However, I did act on her advice and I contacted an agency by letter for adoptees and parents named NORCAP, based in Oxford. I gave them a copy of my birth certificate and asked them to find more information on my birth mother. It took six months before I received any concrete information.

In September I received a letter from Oxford. The letter confirmed the progress of the search and enclosed my mother's marriage certificate. My excitement as I read through the letter was complete elation. Both Judy and I began to believe that we were getting somewhere, yet neither of us knew what the eventual outcome would lead to.

My birth mother married Leonard Frank Bailey in Aylesbury in December 1947. At the time of their marriage, she was twenty-three, so in 1991 she would have been in her sixty-seventh year. The researcher had attempted to trace Leonard Bailey in the Aylesbury area telephone directory, but there was no record.

Fortunately there was a listing under B. E. Bailey which the researcher's cross-checked against the electoral role. Listed on the role was a woman named Bridget Enda Bailey, living in the village of Long Crendon, a few miles from Wotton Underwood. We were onto something – I just couldn't believe my good luck. The letter ended by saying, 'Paul, I guess you may feel a bit overwhelmed by this letter, but I thought it best to let you know what I've found…'[37] Overwhelmed, I was jumping over the moon for joy!

---

[37] Rosalyn Stanley, NORCAP to Paul G. Denny, September 16, 1991.

The details on the electoral role confirmed my mother's postal address. I started to ponder how I would go about making contact. As I reflected on the reality of initiating a process to make contact, I began to realise that for her, the passage of time was going to be a difficult process. For my birth mother, to revisit those memories after so many years would be a great shock. More importantly she may have kept my birth a secret from the rest of her family. I needed an intermediary who could make contact with my mother. The challenge was how to enable that process.

Later that evening I made a calculated guess. If my birth mother was still a practicing Catholic, she would be known as a parishioner at her local church. I contacted the international telephone directory for the nearest Catholic Church in the vicinity of Long Crendon and the operator found there was a church in the village, listing the number for the resident priest. Thanking the operator, I immediately dialled the number and waited for a reply.

A man answered the telephone. 'Good morning, Father Boswell speaking.'

'Good morning, Father. My name is Paul Denny. I'm calling from New Zealand.' I began to tell him the purpose of my phone call, explaining I was adopted in England in 1946 and I was attempting to trace my birth mother. My research indicated my birth mother lived in Long Crendon and as she was a Catholic, she may be a parishioner at the local church. Then I disclosed my birth mother's name and asked anxiously whether he knew her.

The line went dead for what seemed like ages. The priest then replied, speaking in a slow measured voice. 'I do know an Enda Bailey. She helps me with my washing, as I don't have a fulltime housekeeper. I'm not sure it's a good idea for you to make contact with her. It's been a long time and your mother would be shocked to hear from you after so many years.' He ended with a tone of trepidation in his voice, implying it would be preferable not to pursue the matter further.

My immediate response was to acknowledge it would be a great shock for her to hear from me after so many years. However, I had given the subject a great deal of thought. I explained many adopted people attempted to find more information concerning their birth and if my birth mother was willing, I would like to establish contact with her. I believed a trusted intermediary was essential to facilitate the process; to give my birth mother the opportunity of either accepting, or rejecting my offer while maintaining her privacy. I suggested to the priest I would write a letter to my mother, care of him, and asked if he would give my letter to her.

The priest replied cautiously, 'I still don't think it's a good idea – let sleeping dogs lie, is what I always say.'

I ignored the sentiment he advocated and stressed again how important for me initiating contact was. In particular, I emphasised the circumstance of my adoption was not of my own choosing; I didn't ask to be adopted, it was my birth right to know. If my mother did not want to make contact, then she could explain her reasons to me by letter. By taking this approach, it would give her space to think on how best to deal with my request. I realised immediately after I stopped speaking to the priest it was a long shot. I had never felt so assertive before.

Father Boswell seemed to accept the logic of my argument and agreed to pass the letter to her.

'When I receive your letter,' the priest said, 'I'll put the envelope inside the washing basket.'

What a strange thing to do, I thought. But on reflection it made the process easier for him, so I just said, 'Thanks Father, I really appreciate your help.'

As I put down the telephone, I realised Father Boswell was less than happy with his decision. He made no comment on whether my letter would result in my birth mother accepting, or rejecting my invitation. Likewise, he gave me no advice, or encouragement; he just accepted with reservations participating in the process.

My next task was to draft a letter to Father Boswell, confirming our agreement. As I started to write to the priest, the realisation that my mother was alive began to sink in. She was married, and most likely would have adult children from that relationship and maybe grandchildren too. Many people would be affected by my action. I proceeded, because whatever the outcome, I just had to know.

What was I going to say in my letter to her? The letter had to be from my heart. I began my letter by explaining I had been adopted in 1946 by two wonderful people, who acted as my parents. They had told me my original birth name, but had little information on my background, except my birth mother was Irish and her surname was McBride. The only other information was my date and place of birth.

Enclosed in the envelope to my birth mother, were photographs of Judy and our children. I was concerned my letter would be a great shock for her and I was once again very conscious my birth may not be known to any of her family. That was the reason my letter to her was sent in confidence to Father Boswell, to act as an intermediary. My letter closed with the words, '...this letter has, I'm sure, brought you some pain, but more importantly I sincerely hope it has also brought you some peace and joy. I do hope you will contact me.'

In my cover letter to Father Boswell, I reiterated my previous proposition on the importance of giving my birth mother the option on how to handle my invitation to make contact. I left the envelope addressed to my birth mother open. In my letter to Father Boswell, I invited him to read the letter to my mother before giving it to her. Concluding, I asked for his understanding and prayers for a successful outcome for both parties. That evening I took the envelope to the post box with a feeling of trepidation. Once the letter was in the post, my fate was sealed. Either I would hear nothing, receive a rejection, or the acceptance that I had always longed for.

***

As I waited apprehensively for a reply, I took the opportunity to write to Elaine Brunner at Wotton House. I apologised for my long delay in writing and filled her in on the progress I had made in tracing my birth mother. I wrote to NORCAPP as well, thanking them for all their assistance. I informed them I now had sufficient information to continue the search without their backing.

The next few days past slowly and the waiting made me very agitated. I had wonderful support from Judy and the children, as they were curious to know what the outcome of my search would disclose. After two weeks I began to think I would hear nothing more. Maybe the letter had not arrived, or Father Boswell had changed his mind and not proceeded with his commitment. Perhaps my mother didn't aspire to the same sentiments I was seeking. I began to think what further steps I should take.

It must have been three weeks since I had posted the letter to the priest in Long Crendon. Saturdays were busy with activities and Judy and the children were away from the house. I decided both lawns needed cutting. After mowing the back lawn, I moved to the front of the house and started to mow the large lawn at the front.

Cycling down the road towards me was the postman. Our post box was mounted at the foot of our driveway and I stopped working and shouted out, 'Anything for us?'

He smiled and looked down at the red canvas pannier mounted in front of the handlebars. 'Nothing much today

I'm afraid,' he said, handing me a light blue airmail envelope.

'Thanks,' I said, as he carried on towards the next house.

I looked at the postmark; it was from England. I rushed back into the house, tore open the envelope and read the letter.

My dear Son & Family,

I can't tell you how happy I am to have got your most welcome letter. You have never left my thoughts. I have always prayed you would be cared for.

I could not keep you 46 years ago, without a home to take you to, but by your (remarks) in your letter I think you already understood that...

My love to you all, your loving mother,

Enda xx[38]

As I continued to read, the tears just poured down my face. All those years had passed when we both carried the burden of not knowing what had happened to each other. The tone of her letter and the joy she expressed knowing I was well cared for made me feel I had always known her.

In her letter she confirmed her husband had died three years earlier. He was aware of my birth at the time of her marriage, as was my mother's younger sister. My letter had been placed in the washing bag, as promised by Father Boswell. When Mother opened my letter, she said she

---

[38] Bridget Enda Bailey to Paul G. Denny, October 12, 1991.

thought she was dreaming. The letter continued expressing her delight in also having a daughter in-law and two new grandchildren. She would reciprocate and look out some family photographs and send them to me. As the letter ended, she told me I had three half-brothers and a half-sister. Even at this early stage, the feeling of belonging was overwhelming.

I had never felt like this before. The only doubts I had were how Mother would tell her family about our reunion and how she would accomplish it. I need not have worried. The telephone rang a few days later.

Picking up the phone, I had not anticipated who the caller might me. Before I could say anything, a woman's voice with a lilting Irish brogue said. 'Is that you, Paul? It's your Mother from Long Crendon.'

'Hello, Mother,' I replied, warmly. I was so bowled over; I was initially unable to find the words to express my delight. Her voice and tone sounded so natural; as if she had been speaking to me for years.

We carried on talking for nearly an hour. I quickly realised how her good-natured, outgoing conversation was her natural forte. Her sincerity was the defining quality of her personality. It was so strange to hear the rhythmic swing of her Irish accent and her repetitive use of the expression, *my son!* The central thread of that wonderful conversation kept leading back to the guilt she had felt over the years, not being able to tell anybody about me, except her husband and her sister Una, keeping it a secret from others for so many years. Her worst fear, she told me, was not knowing what had happened to her child. Was he well-looked after? Did he prosper and find happiness in his future life? For both of us the anguish of the unknown fell away.

Mother dreaded telling her children of my birth, as she felt they would not understand. Her worst fear was they would reproach her for what occurred back in 1945. Fortunately, she had the courage to tell her children a few days after receiving my letter. They were all delighted to know they had other family in New Zealand and shared Mother's sense of relief in not having to continue protecting the secret any longer.

I finished the telephone call, explaining my adoptive parents were not well and I had decided not to tell them about finding her. She made no response to my disclosure. I guess that it was my decision and it was too early in our journey together to discuss my discovery with my parents. We agreed to an exchange of letters between us, enabling both of us to get to know each other. We began a process of exchanging letters fortnightly.

In my second letter, I confirmed that Judy and I had planned to visit England the following year, intentionally to visit Mum and Dad. When Mother heard we were both coming to Britain, her delight and enthusiasm at the prospect of meeting each other in person became as acute as mine.

Over the next few months, Mother and I exchanged letters and photographs, and I also started corresponding with my new-found siblings. The feelings we expressed in our letters began to shape our understanding of each other's parallel lives. During the first few months of 1992, I became conscious of the way I addressed my birth mother. It seemed the natural thing to do was to call her Mother, and not to refer to her as "Mum". In many ways this was out of respect for my adopted mother Dora, whilst recognising Enda, as my birth mother.

In February I received a belated reply to my letter to Elaine Brunner. She apologised for not responding to my letter in September of the previous year, but she had mislaid it. Ironically, Mrs Brunner knew Mother's brother in-law. His brother had married my mother. I replied, giving her the good news that I had made contact. Her reply prompted an idea. Why didn't my Mother and I agree to meet in September 1992, in the grounds of Wotton House?

***

Although the experience of finding my mother was nothing short of exhilarating, life was tinged with sadness and guilt, because Mum and Dad's health continued to deteriorate simultaneously. I had made the conscious decision earlier not to inform Mum and Dad of my search intentions, due to their ill health. There was another reason.

According to research, the motivational pattern of not disclosing the decision to search emanates from "anxiety most adoptees have about their adoptive parent's reaction to search."[39] Karen March argues this conundrum raises questions on "how the adoptive parent-child relationship is affected by the pretence, closed and suspicion awareness contexts created when adoptees search, establish contact, or meet their birth mother without informing or including their adoptive parents."[40] Anecdotal evidence obtained during the 1980's and 1990's suggests, "between 30% and 65% of adopted persons expressed a strong desire to search or were actually searching for their birth parents."[41] Research conducted in Canada during the late 1980's has claimed that 35% of adult adoptees responded positively to questions on their meeting with "the relative with whom they were first united and their feelings of emotional

---

[39] Karen March. "The Dilemma of Adoption Reunion: Establishing Open Communication between Adoptees and Their Birth Mothers." *Family Relations* 46, no. 2 (1997): p. 101.

[40] ibid, p. 102.

[41] Ulrich Muller and Barbara Perry. "Adopted Persons' Search for and Contact with Their Birth Parents I." *Adoption Quarterly* 4, no. 3 (2001): p. 9.

closeness was seen as *close*."[42] Recent evidence, obtained in the early 2000's from countries that practice a regime of open adoption records, indicates around 50% of all adoptees will search for their biological parents at some time in their life.[43] It is interesting to bring into context that research conducted in the 1960's and 1970's suggests, "Adopted children and parents generally had a great deal of difficulty talking about adoption."[44]

[42] James Gladstone and Anne Westhues. "Adoption Reunions: A New Side to Intergenerational Family Relationships." *Family Relations* 47, no. 2 (1998): p. 179.

[43] Ulrich Muller and Barbara Perry. "Adopted Persons' Search for and Contact with Their Birth Parents I." *Adoption Quarterly* 4, no. 3 (2001): p. 20.

[44] ibid, p. 12.

Chapter 10

We confirmed our plans to visit England during the end of summer 1992. The exchange of letters between Mother and me continued and gradually we began to get to know each other. I made the decision to keep all the letters she sent; perhaps subconsciously the motivation was in case I lost contact with her again. Mother did the same, all kept in an old shoe box, just in case.

Judy and I left Auckland for England on the 10th of August. The day before we departed, a letter arrived from Long Crendon. It was Mother, writing to reconfirm our first meeting. We had previously confirmed our itinerary some months before, but the tone of her letter reflected her absolute joy and enthusiasm. She said, 'Yes my dear, the 2nd of September 1992, that's our great day. I will be up on that morning, before the birds...'

We arranged to stay with Judy's twin sister Janet and her husband Albert. They lived in Wokingham, which was ideally situated to travel, both to visit mum and dad in Fairford and Mother and her daughter Frances who lived together in Long Crendon.

The first few days after we had arrived in England, were spent enjoying the hospitality extended by my in-laws. For Judy, staying with her twin sister was always a special occasion and we were fortunate that we all enjoyed each other's company.

Wokingham is only a few miles from Windsor Castle and the four of us revisited once again the splendour of Windsor and the surrounding Royal Park. On most days we enjoyed daily walks together, usually finishing at lunchtime and visiting a country pub. Judy and Janet would go shopping together, often to Marks & Spencer to secure the latest bargain. Albert and I joined them occasionally, preferring to otherwise chat away from the bustle of retail therapy. Most evenings were spent lazily either sitting in their garden followed by an alfresco barbeque, or dining inside if the English weather adhered to its traditional reputation.

I had phoned Mum and Dad as soon as we arrived in Wokingham. We agreed that Judy and I would travel to Fairford at the beginning of our third week. Our plan was to stay in Fairford for two weeks, helping Mum and Dad as much as we could. The journey took little over an hour, and travelling along the pleasant meandering country roads in our small hire car, allowed us to enjoy the sight of many of the autumn trees shedding their yellow leaves. As we drove through the undulating Berkshire countryside, the glitter of numerous patchwork fields teased the morning sunlight; some lying fallow green, others bright with yellow rape flowers. Larger fields had to wait patiently for red combine harvesters to do their work.

As we crossed the county boundary into Gloucestershire, the scenery gradually began to alter. The red-brick houses familiar in Berkshire changed. Now we saw houses built of solid limestone and the fields in pasture appeared greener than those supported by the white chalk limestone of the previous county. As we drove nearer to Fairford, the familiar sight of dry-stone walls, protecting ancient fields, confirmed we were now in the heart of the Cotswolds. Each village has its ancient stone church, encircled with artisan cottages and grander homes. Many of the buildings are protected from the elements by steep-pitched roofs of stone tile, supported by sturdy limestone walls. The elements have painted most of them in darker colours and nature has applied a pallet of grey lichen and moss.

We parked our car as close as we could to Mum and Dad's small house. I pulled the case behind me as we walked towards their house. When we reached their front door, I lifted the familiar black door knocker. Inside Mum's face appeared behind the small glass window set in the door. The front door opened and Mum's beaming smile welcomed us.

'Hello Judy, how are you, dear? It's wonderful to see you again,' she said, warmly hugging her.

'Hi Mum, give us a hug! Great to see you again,' I said embracing her affectionately.

'Don't stand outside, you two. Come in and let's have a cup of tea,' she said predictably, as we walked through the small entrance hall into the lounge.

Dad was not sitting in his favourite chair. Judy and I sat on the small settee. 'You don't drink tea, do you Judy – I always forget dear,' she said, walking towards the small adjacent kitchen. 'Would you like a cup of coffee instead?'

'Yes please Mum, not too strong though,' answered Judy.

'How's Dad keeping, Mum?' I asked, remembering Dad was in respite at the local hospital for a few days. 'What do the doctors say?'

Mum brought our tea and coffee into the lounge and sat down. Leaning back into her favourite armchair, she began to drink her tea. As I looked across towards her, I realised how much older she looked since I had last seen her.

'As you both know dear, Dad's been in and out of respite, every few weeks. Neither of us is as young as we were. The doctors and nurses are wonderful. They aren't really sure what they can do for Dad, though. His eyesight's failing and his heart is not as strong as it was.'

I knew Dad's health was deteriorating fast and Mum was bearing the brunt of it too. Judy and I felt so helpless.

'Mum, when can we go and see Dad?' I said. 'We could all walk down together. It saves us going by car.'

'Why don't we leave at around eleven o'clock?' Mum replied. 'The staff let me visit anytime. Dad will be so glad to see you both.'

We all walked down to the village square, stopping at the only flower shop in the village. I bought a small bunch of flowers.

'Dad, will appreciate those,' Mum said, tongue in cheek. 'The florist is making a fortune out of us!'

As we entered the reception area of the hospital, a friendly female voice spoke from behind the desk.

'Morning Mrs Denny, your husband's got *three* visitors today – lucky man!'

'Yes – he's so looking forward to seeing us. This is my son and daughter in-law. They're on holiday from New Zealand,' Mum replied.

'How nice for you both,' the receptionist said. 'I hope you enjoy your stay in England. I've always wanted to visit New Zealand.' We all smiled politely back.

'You can all go straight in, Mrs Denny,' said the receptionist and I pushed open the swing doors leading towards the ward area.

Dad was in a small ward for male geriatrics. The room felt repressive and the heat from the radiators felt as if they were full-on. There were eight beds in the ward, four of which looked outside onto an enclosed quadrangle. The courtyard was laid with lawn and edged with standard roses, providing a welcome connection with the world outside. In the centre of the lawn was a stone bird-bath and a red-breasted robin was standing on the edge, enjoying a welcome drink.

Mum led us towards Dad's single bed at the far end of the ward. It also faced out towards the courtyard. Dad looked as if he was asleep, but his eyes kept opening as if he was just dozing. Mum sat down to the left of the bed. Judy and I secured two other chairs and sat on the other side. I placed the flowers on the bedside table and turned towards him.

'Hi Dad, how are you keeping?' I asked in a cheerful voice. The sound of my voice startled him and his eyes began to open.

'Hello Paul,' he said, turning his head slowly towards Judy and me. 'I'm not too bad Laddie – when did you two arrive?' he asked, his head leaning back onto the raised pillow, his breathing very light and uneven.

'We both arrived this morning Dad,' said Judy, moving closer and giving him a big hug. We've been staying with my sister in Wokingham.'

'You're looking very well,' Dad replied, slowly. 'Did you have a good journey over from Auckland?'

'Yes, Dad,' she said. 'We travelled via Singapore. You and Mum liked it there, didn't you?'

'That was a while ago, Judy,' he said, his eyes beginning to close again.

I hadn't seen Dad for eighteen months. As he lay back in the bed, he looked a frail and tired old man. His face was drawn and pale. I had never seen him like that. I was shocked, but tried not to show it.

His eyes began to open again and Mum asked him if he had seen the doctors that morning. He replied slowly, 'Yes darling, they said they're going to let me go home at the weekend.'

That's great news, darling,' said Mum. 'Paul and Judy will be staying with us next week as well.'

We stayed and chatted for an hour and Dad continued to look frail.

'Darling, Paul and Judy have left you some flowers,' Mum said to Dad.

He looked back towards us, but didn't reply. His eyes began to close again and Mum asked. 'Paul, please ask one of those kind nurses to put those lovely flowers in some water?'

'Sure Mum,' I said, walking out into the corridor to find a nurse who could assist.

When I returned, we said our farewells to Dad. We were all conscious our visit had exhausted him. Mum and Judy gave Dad a hug. I leaned down and squeezed his frail left hand. We all said we would come in the next day to visit him and we waved goodbye. He returned the gesture meekly, waving his hand towards us as we left the ward.

On Saturday morning the ambulance brought Dad home. The medics manoeuvred him into his wheelchair and into the house. He looked exhausted as he lay back in his favourite fireside chair.

'Who wants a cup of tea or coffee?' said Mum.

Judy and I opted for coffee. Dad moved his lips in a silent gesture, indicating his choice was tea. We all sat back and enjoyed our refreshments, but after a few minutes he was looking very tired. Dad looked upwards, indicating he wanted to rest in bed. Judy and I helped him reach the base of the stairs.

Accepting the inevitable, Mum had arranged to install a chair lift the year before, providing easy access to the first floor. With great difficulty Dad managed to seat himself onto the chair lift. I pressed the red button and the lift made its way gradually upwards towards the bedroom landing.

During that visit to Fairford, most of our time and effort was spent nursing Dad. Fortunately, he received care from the district nurse, who called in every day. This gave Mum support, as now in her eightieth year, she was getting frail. Judy and I were worried, not just for Dad, but the effect his illness was having on her own health.

There was little we could really do to help. We both helped Mum with cooking and general household tasks and Judy ably assisted Mum in the nursing care role. By the end of the second week he was transferred back to the hospital. In a way this was a blessing for Mum, as she needed time to rest.

Once Dad was settled back in the ward, Mum, Judy and I walked down to visit him. When we arrived at the hospital, he was predictably asleep and remained so during our stay. I noticed his breathing was again shallow and irregular. Mum retained her composure, although she must have realised how serious Dad's state of health had now become. I began to acknowledge the obvious; Dad was seriously ill.

We left Fairford the following morning. Mum was sad to see us depart, but understood we needed to spend time with family in Wokingham, as well as Judy's mother who lived in Birmingham. Before leaving Fairford, I promised Mum to spend my final week in England with her. Judy had planned to travel back to Auckland alone at the end of September, as she wanted to stay and celebrate her birthday in Wokingham with her twin sister.

The next week I planned to drive to Thame, a small market town close to Long Crendon. I booked a room at The Spread Eagle Hotel, although Mother had asked me to stay with her. It somehow didn't seem right to stay with her before I had actually met her in person. Wednesday the 2nd of September was the day I would meet my mother face to face; it was so sad I wasn't able to share it with my Mum and Dad.

***

I arrived in Thame shortly after nine, having left Wokingham at eight o'clock. The drive westwards through the Thames Valley tracked the meandering River Thames for much of the journey and the traffic fortunately was light. I parked briefly outside the hotel in Thame, reconfirmed my reservation at the desk and was back inside my vehicle in less than five minutes. To say I was in a hurry would have been an understatement.

Mother and I had agreed to meet in the village of Wotton Underwood at ten o'clock. Throughout the early morning journey, my mind was absorbed totally on how I would feel, when we finally met again, after forty-six years apart. We had of course exchanged photographs of each other and our families. We had spoken to each other many times on the telephone. Yet, to meet again in the flesh, many chapters later in our lives were unknown territory for us both. I could only wildly speculate on what I would say and how I would feel. Mother must have been feeling the same.

Wotton Underwood is dominated by its ancient church and its Georgian manor houses. I arrived fifteen minutes early, parking the car close to the churchyard entrance. Scattered close to the church are a few small cottages, with other similar properties situated along the approach road to the village. Mother didn't drive and my sister Frances had kindly agreed to drive her from their home in Long Crendon, leaving mother and son together to share their special reunion.

I became more anxious as the hour approached and continually kept looking at my wristwatch. My only companions were the birds in the surrounding shrubbery and the sound of a light breeze in the trees. The road into the village came from the south and the solitude of the location was eventually broken by the sound of a car in the distance. My hearing focused on the direction of the vehicle. Coming towards me, was a small white Metro with two people seated in the front.

Instinctively I waved amiably towards the occupants, both of whom returned the gesture somewhat meekly. The car stopped a few metres from where I was standing. Frances parked the car and walked towards me.

'Hello Paul, it's great to meet you at last,' she said.

'Hello Frances,' I replied. 'I've certainly taken my time over it!'

We hugged each other for a few seconds and then both of us turned towards the car. Mother was still sitting in the passenger seat with her head facing downwards and a handkerchief clutched between her hands.

'Paul, Mum's a bit overcome with emotion, as you'd expect,' said Frances.

Frances opened the passenger door and Mother looked up with a subdued smile. Slowly she began getting out of the car. I moved towards her. We both embraced. Both of us just stood, holding each other, lost for words.

'I'll leave you two together then,' Frances said tactfully, appreciating our mutual need for private space.

Frances got back into the driving seat and started the engine. Winding down the window she looked out of the car.

Leaving me, Frances asked, 'look after Mum, see you two back at the house after lunch. Bye for now.'

The car sped away and we were still locked in our initial embrace. We were beyond tears of joy. The sense of absolute peace we enjoyed at that moment was broken by me.

'Mother, it's so wonderful to hold you and feel your physical presence – it's been a long time.' She didn't reply with words, she didn't need too. We both stood back and looked at each other. Her face radiated with affection.

'I hope we weren't too late Paul,' she said anxiously in her soft Irish brogue. Placing her hand in mine, we started to walk. 'Let me show you the house where I worked all those years ago.'

We walked away from the churchyard towards Wotton House. I recall how she took the lead, let go of my hand and preceded me along the public footpath leading up towards the house. By taking the lead, the gesture demonstrated to me a mother's natural instinct and that she knew the way. I happily followed her along the short pathway, leading along the edge of a fenced field. Inside were scattered sheep, feeding contentedly on early autumn pasture.

Following her up the path gave me time to gather my thoughts. What struck me was how ingenuous our close proximity felt. It was as if we had never been apart. Our initial embrace felt like two lost jigsaw pieces finally reassembled.

As we continued walking, I couldn't stop Mother talking – it was just wonderful to hear all that held back emotion come pouring out. The Irish have a reputation for rhetoric – she certainly demonstrated that gift. I could hardly get a word in edgeways – it didn't matter a bit.

As the great house came into view, Mother pointed out where she had lived. 'Paul, that's my room up there,' she said, pointing to a small window on the top floor of the building. 'All the workers lived in attic rooms at the top of the house. Not that any of us had much time for leisure in those days. We all worked from early morning till night-time and each of us only had one day off during the week. My sister and I came over from Waterford during the war. I worked for Major Beaumont and his wife who owned the house.'

I couldn't get a word in. Mother just continued talking; there was so much to say. I listened eagerly to the rhythm of her voice. The Irish brogue, with its soft vowels and hard consonants washed over me. The sound of her voice helped to soften the hurt and isolation I had felt from those years apart. I sensed she needed to take the lead; to set the tone of the conversation. She repeated continually the sentiment expressed earlier, when she first wrote to me. The regret she had carried with her all those years; not knowing how I had fared and the guilt she felt not being able to care for me herself. A mother's natural regret was slowly unwinding.

After seeing the manor house, I suggested we find a local country pub for lunch to celebrate our reunion. Mother recommended a pub close to Long Crendon and we both got into the car. Like a couple of young teenagers; we laughed and giggled, until we arrived at The Angel.

As I went to order our drinks, Mother sat down at a small table for two. As bold as brass she began to engage with a few other patrons who were quietly enjoying their drinks.

'That's my eldest son from New Zealand!' she declared proudly as the customers smiled back, somewhat surprised. 'I haven't seen him for forty-six years.' She looked at me with a beaming smile, while I stood at the bar. I smiled back ineptly towards Mother and the other patrons drinking in the bar. As I paid for the drinks and brought them to our table, she reiterated once again the same remark, 'I haven't seen him for forty-six years.'

Being able to disclose the secret of her past put a spring in her step; she wanted to broadcast the fact to everybody, absolving herself of any sense of guilt. Watching her so supremely joyful made me feel so very happy. I'll never forget it.

After we had finished our lunch, we left The Angel and drove back to her home in Long Crendon. The process of really getting to know each other was just beginning. Frances met us as Mother inserted her key into the front door, and within minutes we were all sitting in the dining room, looking out towards the back garden. Predictably, Mother used the standard British welcome; 'Who wants a nice cup of tea then? To which the siblings replied, 'Yes please, Mother!'

That evening I met my youngest brother Vincent and his wife Margaret. I was introduced to their young daughter Anna, as Uncle Paul. All of us were naturally curious about each other, yet we all accepted the reality of what had occurred all those years ago. It was another chapter in all our lives and everyone surprisingly embraced the opportunity. That evening I went back to sleep at The Spread Eagle Hotel.

The following night I slept at Mother's house. I had planned to extend my accommodation at the hotel, as I felt Mother and Frances may feel obliged in providing me with accommodation. These were early days and I didn't wish to overstep my welcome. To me, my reticence seemed a natural emotion. Their house was their home, not mine, and I was a guest. Predictably, Mother kept referring to *her* home as *our* home, which was a very kind sentiment, prompted by her maternal desire to make me feel welcome. I welcomed her good intentions and kindness, but always respected that the house in Long Crendon was their property and not *my* home.

The next morning I drove to Wokingham and returned to Long Crendon with Judy. We decided to spend the day at Burnham Beeches, an ancient tract of woodland in Buckinghamshire. Ironically, it was a place I used to walk many years earlier. The venue gave Judy and me the opportunity of meeting Mother, Frances and Vince and his family in a natural environment.

Mother quickly established a warm relationship with Judy. Her lead encouraged the rest of the family to engage with their newly acquired family from Down Under. After spending a wonderful day together, we said our farewells. I had told Mother I needed to return to Wokingham. Mother instinctively understood the dilemma I was experiencing and the importance of revisiting Mum and Dad, before I departed for Auckland on September the 25th.

***

The next ten days were spent in Wokingham, as Judy was keen to spend the rest of her visit with her twin sister. We both enjoyed our time together, but in the back of our minds were our concerns for Mum and Dad in Fairford. I'd promised Mum I would spend the last seven days of my holiday in the Cotswolds. I left Judy in Wokingham and drove over to Fairford.

When I arrived, Mum was cleaning the house. Dad was in respite again at the local hospital, which gave Mum and me the opportunity to spend some quality time together. Every day we visited Dad; both in the morning and early evening. His breathing had deteriorated since I saw him some weeks before, yet we all optimistically hoped for an improvement. Mum was a tower of strength as always, yet I detected that she also was experiencing some health issue. I asked her how she was coping with Dad and how her own health was holding up. 'I'm just fine Paul,' she replied stoically. 'I have had some tests done; the doctor was concerned I wasn't eating as well as I should be.'

I knew from the tone of her voice and the expression of denial on her face her answer was less than truthful. She always thought firstly of others and seldom of herself. Mum then turned the conversation away from her own concerns and began to talk about Dad.

'Dad's more comfortable in hospital,' she said. 'Although Dad being Dad, he always wants to come straight home, immediately after he's admitted.'

'I suppose that's natural,' I said. 'We all want to get back home when we don't feel well.'

I then looked straight at Mum and said.

'You need to look after yourself as well Mum. When do you expect the results?' She didn't reply immediately. When she did a few seconds later, she avoided direct eye contact. 'Next week with a bit of luck dear – they do tend to fuss a bit, don't they?'

I avoided pursuing her indirect question. We visited Dad twice a day and after Thursday's early evening visit, Mum and I planned to drive out for dinner.

'I thought we might go out for a meal on my last night, Mum. You always enjoyed the grilled trout at the Masons Arms,' I said, knowing she would succumb easily to the temptation.

We visited Dad on Thursday around six-thirty. He was in better spirits than I had seen him all week and he was propped up with two large pillows. He had been reading.

I told him, 'Dad – I'm taking Mum out for dinner tonight. I thought we'd go to the Masons Arms.'

Dad didn't look in the least surprised.

'Your Mum will want the trout I expect. Won't you, dear?' he said, smiling broadly.

'I expect I will darling, you know me. It's my favourite,' Mum replied, without expressing much enthusiasm, to avoid making the prospect of our evening out look too attractive.

'We won't be staying late though, will we Paul?'

There was no need to reply to her question. Mum had inadvertently framed the question, so as to not make Dad too resentful.

238

Looking slowly across to the clock on his bedside cabinet, Dad said. 'You two don't want to be late, do you?'

Neither Mum nor I replied. It was time to say goodnight. Mum leaned across and kissed him gently. 'We'll come and see you tomorrow darling.'

'Have a nice evening,' he said, leaning slowly back against his pillow.

I moved over towards him and gave him a long hug. He was more lucid than I had seen him all week. 'Dad – I am leaving Fairford tomorrow – I fly back to Auckland on Friday. I'll come in to see you before I leave,' I said. I could see in his eyes he was beginning to get tired, it was time for us to go.

'Look after Mum, won't you,' he said, his eyes beginning to gradually close. I somehow felt he meant longer than just this evening.

'I promise, Dad,' I replied, but he was asleep.

We both stood up in silence and began to quietly slip away from his bedside.

'Sleep well, darling,' said Mum softly, as we left the ward.

***

The drive to the Masons Arms took less than ten minutes. 'Dad looked a lot better tonight,' I said, as we climbed into the car.

'He was certainly much more cheerful dear. I do hope he sleeps well tonight,' Mum said, tightening her seat belt securely.

By seven thirty we were seated in the Mason Arms. The pub is on the main road running through the village of Down Ampney. I had visited the village many times before, often with Mum and Dad. Possessing a beautiful stone church, the village has links back to the bubonic plague in the fourteenth century, which decimated the population of Europe. Fortunately, times had changed and we found a comfortable table for two, close to a window, facing the highway.

The day's specials were listed on the chalk board.

'Going for the rainbow trout, Mum?' I asked, while I scanned the menu, not having made my own mind up.

'Yes please dear, I'd like the fish grilled – with the mixed vegetables, please.'

'What would you like to drink Mum?' I asked, pointing to a popular Chardonnay on the menu card. I was happy to buy a bottle, but I knew she would just prefer to have wine by the glass.

'That sounds like a good idea,' she said, taking up my recommendation. 'Just a small glass though.'

'I fancy a pint of ale, Mum,' I said, as I got up from the table to place our order at the bar. Like many pubs in the area, the landlord prided himself on carrying at least four guest beers.

'Eating with us tonight, Sir?' asked the barman, as I ordered our drinks.

'Yes, A glass of Chardonnay and a pint of best please.' As he poured our drinks, I asked him what he recommended on the menu.

'The eye fillet is good, if you like a good steak, Sir,' the barman replied.

'Yes, thanks,' I replied. 'That sounds great – my mother's going to have the trout.'

'Sir, how would you like your steak cooked?' he asked, writing up the order.

'Rare please and jacket potatoes with mixed vegetables too.'

'And the lady sir? – You said rainbow trout – grilled or baked, was it?'

'Grilled please, with mixed vegetables,' I replied.

After he had taken the order, I placed my credit card on the bar, paying for the two meals and drinks. I returned to our table with my pint of best and the glass of Chardonnay.

'Thank you dear,' she said appreciatively, as I placed her glass on the table.

'Cheers Mum,' I said, lifting my glass.

'Cheers– I do wish Dad had been able to be with us this evening,' she said, as we clinked our glasses together.

Our dinner arrived after a short wait.

'Would you like another glass of wine, Mum?' I asked, as the waitress waited in anticipation

'I shouldn't really, should I dear?' she replied.

I looked up towards the young waitress. 'Could we have another glass of Chardonnay and a pint of best please?'

'The fish looks nice,' I said, as she picked up her knife and fork.

As I began to slice into my steak, she replied. 'It's delicious dear; we must come here again, next time you come over to visit.'

The poignancy of her remark suddenly struck me. Dad's health was in steep decline and Mum's prognosis on her health was uncertain. It seemed like an opportunity to share what was happening with my birth mother and how wonderful it would have been to share it with her. We might never get the chance again.

As I rationalised the logic of what my response would be, I realised I was beginning to forget the reason I had kept the secret of my new encounter away from them. With all their health problems, in the twilight of their lives, my discovery just would not add anything positive to their predicament. That was the logic – but deep inside I wish I'd had the courage to share the news with them.

Our conversation at the pub was special. Very seldom had we spent time together just socialising. Mum and Dad had enjoyed their leisure time with friends, or family within a group. One on one encounters were not the norm. We spent most of the time discussing the grandchildren and Mum indicated she would love to come to New Zealand again for a holiday. I took that to mean alone, when Dad eventually passed away. It was a strange thing to say during dinner and I didn't comment other than to say Judy and I would be delighted. Mum was in good heart, although I knew she regretted my imminent departure for New Zealand the following morning. Once we had finished eating, Mum suggested we had coffee back at her house.

The next morning I rose early, as did Mum. We had breakfast together and once I had finished my packing, we both left the house and walked to the hospital to say my final farewell to Dad. The normally peaceful walk through the village between eight and nine was interrupted by the noise of heavy traffic. The planned bypass skirting the small town was scheduled for construction when Mum and Dad had retired to Fairford twenty years previously. Like many capital work projects, budgets had been cut, or priorities redefined, yet the volume of traffic through similar communities, built for horse and cart, never receded.

Dad had finished eating breakfast when we entered the ward and the staff had moved him to a comfortable high back chair. He was dressed in pyjamas, covered by his old fawn dressing gown. Other patients were seated in similar chairs and many of them displayed symptoms of dementia. Dad raised his right arm slowly and waved as we both came closer. Mum and I secured two side chairs, moving them close to where he was seated.

'Hello Dad. How are you feeling today?' I asked optimistically, giving his hand a gently squeeze.

'Not too bad Laddie,' he said, with a hint of resignation in his voice. He looked tired as Mum kissed him.

'Hello darling,' she said. 'Paul and I had a lovely evening last night. The trout was delicious – as always.'

'We always liked that place, didn't we dear?' he replied slowly. 'Paul, what did you have to eat?'

'You know me Dad – I had a steak as usual. No chips though; trying to stay healthy,' I replied.

'Bet you had a pint though!' Dad said, with a kind glint in his eyes.

We stayed chatting for around half an hour. By the end of our visit, Dad, as usual, was beginning to get exhausted.

'Darling, Paul needs to be on his way soon. He doesn't want to miss his flight, does he?' she said, as she turning towards me.

'No Mum, I had better get going. I've got to take the hire car back, before I join the queue at Terminal 3. I don't want to be late.'

Dad turned towards me leaning forward slightly in his chair. I squeezed my hands tightly again around his frail hands.

'Dad, I'd better be going then.'

'Well, once again Laddie,' he said, trying to sound in control. 'Mum and I are going to miss you – take great care of yourself. Love to Judy and the children. Let us both know you're safe when you get back home?'

'I will Dad, take care,' I said, moving closer. As I reached over to give him a long hug, I said, 'Dad, I love you so much – take care.'

We held each other for a few more moments before I let him go. He sank back into the chair, his eyes looking down towards the floor. As Mum and I left the ward, we waved. His head had turned and he just stared, waving one hand towards us. Seeing him next to other geriatric patients, each with their own struggling attempts to survive reinforced the finality of the encounter. I managed to hold my tears of sadness back. Dad would not have expected anything less. Inside though, I think Dad and I recognised it would be the last time we would ever see each other.

We walked back to the house and Mum and I hardly spoke. I went upstairs and retrieved my suitcase.

'Are you leaving straight away, Paul?' Mum asked despondently, after I returned downstairs. 'Can I get you a cup of tea?'

I knew if I stayed any longer it would make it even more difficult to finally say goodbye.

'No thanks, Mum – I'd better get going, like I said to Dad...'

***

I spent the rest of the day in Wokingham with Judy, my brother in-law and Judy's twin. Late in the afternoon I said my fond farewells and drove to Heathrow to catch my early evening flight to Auckland. Our only stop was in Singapore where I could stretch my legs for a couple of hours before the final sector to Auckland. The thirteen hours from London to Singapore gave me time to reflect on the momentous events that had occurred during my visit to England. In reality I managed to sleep for much of the journey, which eased my combination of anxiety and happiness. I had at last met my birth mother; Dad was seriously ill and in a state of decline and I was very worried about Mum's health. To say the least, my emotions were jumbled up and my prime concern was Mum and Dad's welfare. The joy of finding Mother, somehow at this juncture was eclipsed.

Sunday lunchtime, my flight touched down in Auckland. I caught a taxi back home and spent the afternoon trying to get the lawns in shape after so many weeks away. The following morning I didn't feel like breakfast. As usual I had taken advantage of the generous hospitality on board the flight and black coffee was all I needed to sustain myself before lunch.

I had promised to telephone Mum to let her know that I had arrived safely. The best time to phone was in the early evening as it would be Sunday morning in England. I decided to phone Mum at eight in the evening and I spent the rest of the day doing odd jobs around the house. After dinner, I poured myself a large whisky and settled back to enjoy a few hours of television. Predictably, the programmes were less than enthralling and as I went to refill my glass with the amber spirit, the telephone rang.

I picked up the receiver.

'It's Mum here – Is that you, Paul?' I knew immediately from the tone of her voice, something was terribly wrong.

'Dad died a few hours ago,' she said, faintly. Then there was a short silence.

'Oh Mum – I'm so sorry,' I said, trying to hold back my tears. 'What happened?'

Mum continued speaking and as she spoke, her voice began to slowly fall apart.

After a long pause, she began to speak. 'The hospital called me yesterday afternoon, saying Dad was having breathing problems. I dashed down to the ward – Ken and Moiré took me. Dad was on oxygen. The doctors were very worried – his heart was getting weaker. And then, he just slipped away,' she said, finally bursting into tears.

Neither of us could contain ourselves. We both let out our grief, crying together for what seemed like ages.

'Mum, I can come back and help you,' I offered.

'Don't be silly dear,' she said, pulling herself together. 'You've only just seen your Dad – I'll be fine. The neighbours next door have rallied round – I'll be alright, honestly.'

I knew Mum was devastated, but predictably, she rallied as always and gathered the strength to compose herself. I just don't know how she did it; Mum was such a tower of strength. We were both in shock and thinking how I could help Mum was difficult. Mum and Dad had been so fortunate in their retirement together. Over twenty years in Fairford, they acquired many close friends and good neighbours.

'Mum, I just can't believe Dad is really gone.'

'No, neither can I dear – it's just such a shock.'

The tone in her voice gradually strengthened as we continued talking.

'Mum, I'll phone Judy in a few minutes,' I said, attempting to comfort her.

We said our goodbyes, mixed with a few more tears.

'I'll give you a ring tomorrow, Mum – love you so much.'

After exchanging a few more words of comfort, we said goodbye. Before I placed the handset down, all I could hear was the lonely sound of the dial tone.

I telephoned Judy straight away and told her about Dad. She sounded as shocked as I was. We were both in denial about how sick Dad had really been.

'He must have waited until you'd gone,' she said, striving to comfort me.

'You're probably right,' I said. 'We'll never really know.'

We continued talking about Mum's health and my concern over her well-being. Living without Dad would be difficult for her, as they had shared so much over the years. I reminded Judy of the recent conversation Mum and I had at the Masons Arms the week before. During the dinner Mum had alluded to coming out again to Auckland to spend time with us. Judy had always had a very warm relationship with her and welcomed the opportunity of having her stay with us again. Little did I know at the time how prophetic Mum's remarks would be.

Before saying goodbye to Judy, I asked her to phone Mum in Fairford as soon as possible. I explained to Judy I had asked Mum if I should fly back to England. Judy understood Mum's sentiment and said she would attend Dad's funeral on my behalf. We all understood that I had been so fortunate in seeing Dad a few days before he died. Travelling back was not a practical solution. Better to travel later, when Mum's health improved.

***

During October, Mum was taken seriously ill and hospitalised in Oxford. She telephoned me from her bedside to tell me the prognosis – it wasn't the news either of us wanted to hear. When the call came through, the operator at the hospital switchboard announced the call.

'Mr Denny, I have Mrs Denny calling,' he said, connecting me through to Mum's bedside extension. As we exchanged our initial greeting, Mum sounded weak and downhearted.

'How are you keeping Paul? It's wonderful to hear your voice.'

'I'm fine Mum, how are you?' I asked, trying to sound optimistic.

'The doctors can't treat my *condition*,' she said, with the emphasis on *condition*. 'I'm in the oncology ward. Tomorrow, the doctors are sending me back to Fairford.'

Typically, Mum never mentioned the word cancer. Both of us knew what it meant. Mum was going back to die in Fairford Hospital.

Feeling totally devastated, I said. 'Mum – I'll phone you tomorrow evening and see how you are. Is there anything I can do?'

'No, dear. Thanks so much for asking. There's nothing you can do – I just want to get back to Fairford.'

'I'll phone you tomorrow, Mum,' I said, holding back my heartache.

After saying goodbye I started to cry. I felt absolutely gutted.

Over the next few weeks we continued to speak with each other as much as we could. We never discussed the word *cancer*, but the tone and strength of her voice during each phone call confirmed her decline.

I managed to speak with the matron of the hospital in early November, who confirmed my worst fears. Mum had only a short time left to live. By the third week in November I received an urgent call from the hospital. My first question was, 'How's Mum?' knowing what the inevitable reply was likely to be.

The matron answered my question.

'Mr Denny, if you could come over and visit your Mum; *sooner* rather than later would be good? Your Mum is very ill.'

The emphasis on the word *sooner* kept resonating in my ears. I managed somehow to reply, although the tone in my voice denied the finality of her invitation.

248

'Would next week be *good*?' I said naively.

'If you could fly to England tomorrow, that would be *preferable*,' the matron said.

'Please tell mum I will be on a flight tomorrow. I will be with her within two days. Please give her my love?'

'I'll let your mum know you're coming, Mr Denny. She will be so pleased. Perhaps you can let me know what time you will be here.'

'As soon as my flight details are confirmed, I'll phone and let you know. Thanks so much for all your help.' I said, putting down the telephone.

Looking back now, I was so privileged to be able to spend the last week of Mum's life with her in Fairford. My brother-in-law Albert met me at Heathrow early in the morning and drove me straight to Mum's house in Fairford. The November weather was true to form, cold and raining. As we drove along the sombre winding roads towards Fairford, we exchanged few words. The stark winter landscape contrasted against the warmth of the car interior. Outside, the sight of bleak winter trees without their leaves bore a sense of impending demise in my heart.

Mum's empty home felt cold and bleak. The central heating had been turned down low. The only sound was from the refrigerator, some kind neighbour had placed a few essential items of food inside. Mum had given two close neighbours house keys many years previously and I also had retained a key. Albert drove back to Wokingham and I stayed in Fairford for a week.

Shortly after Albert had left, I left Mum's house and walked down quickly to the hospital. She was fortunate to have a single ward and when I entered she was asleep. The warm room was filled with flowers from friends and family and the air was filled with their pungent aroma. I sat by the bed, looking at her drawn, pale face. The only sound was her light irregular breathing. Within a few minutes she stirred and her eyes opened, looking directly towards me.

I stood up and leaned over the bed, kissing her lightly on the cheek. We both smiled and as I moved closer, she attempted to share my embrace. I held her closely; the lightness of her frail frame shocked me. Her head slipped back almost immediately onto the raised pillow, the effort too much to bear.

'Thank you for coming, darling,' she said gratefully, her eyes turning slowly towards the window.

As she gazed outside, she noticed a red robin feeding.

'Paul, look at the robin feeding on the birdbath. I wonder if it's the same one Dad saw?' recalling a similar incident when he was in hospital a few months earlier.

I smiled. 'Maybe, Mum, I hope so.'

We continued to talk about normal everyday things; both of us knew why I was here. I asked her how the doctors and nurses were caring for her and how she felt since arriving back in Fairford.

'I'm so glad to be home,' she said, contentedly. 'The Oxford hospital was far too big. I'm so much happier in Fairford, where I belong.'

Our conversation continued, although there were many times we didn't speak at all. There were long periods of silence; waiting and unspoken reflection. Mum was getting progressively weaker and I knew she was in pain. The sight of her pain pump on the bedspread confirmed she was on morphine. As I sat by her bed, I watched Mum's eyes close as she kept falling asleep. After a while her eyelids flickered and she regained consciousness.

'I'll come down in the afternoon, Mum,' I said softly, as her vacant milky eyes stared directly at me.

Before she had time to respond, her eyes closed again. She'd fallen asleep. I left the room as quietly as I could and walked sadly back to her empty house.

The week progressed and Mum's strength deteriorated. I visited twice each day. The first few days had allowed us to share many of our memories from the past. Each day the morphine masked her pain, but as the days wore on, she slipped into a coma. On Friday afternoon, before my scheduled visit, the hospital phoned. The staff nurse said Mum was quietly slipping away.

I arrived at her bedside within a few minutes. Moira, a close friend and neighbour, was sitting by Mum's bed.

'Hello Paul,' she said quietly, as I sat down opposite. Mum was unconscious and breathing heavily. I'd never before experienced the sound of the death rattle; the low-pitched broken irregular sound, deep from the throat.

I turned towards Moira. 'Shall I call the nurse or the doctor?' I asked in disbelief.

'Dora's not in any pain, Paul, it won't be long,' she said kindly, putting out a hand towards me.

Mum's breathing was noticeably shallower. The only sound was a low-pitched gurgle as Mum finally gave up her spirit. The breathing had stopped; my head fell in to my open hands, my warm tears streamed down my face.

I lost all sense of time and space. Moira came across and placed her arms around me.

'I'm so sorry Paul – I'll go and see if I can find the charge-nurse,' she said, quietly leaving the room.

After Moira had left, I looked up towards the bed. Mum's still body was lying composed; silent, alone, at peace. Her eyelids were closed and I moved towards her face and gave her a final gentle kiss goodbye.

The doctor came shortly and certified her death. I stayed with her for an hour after she died and her physical presence remained within the room, until just before I left the ward.

Shortly after Mum died, Moira telephoned her husband Ken, asking him to come down to the hospital. The three of us later left the hospital and walked back to their cottage, opposite Mum's house. Even with their kind support, the walk was the loneliest I have ever undertaken.

I don't know how I would have handled the trauma of Mum's death without Ken and Moira's support. Although they both encouraged me to stay with them for as long as I needed, I knew I wanted to return to Mum's house and be alone. The reality of her passing was beginning to sink in. Later that evening I phoned a local funeral director. He arranged to collect Mum's body from the hospital and suggested the funeral would be on the following Friday.

The next week was spent contacting Mum's friends. Their love and support were invaluable to me. Every day I took long walks alone in the countryside. It helped to slowly heal my grief. During that week I reflected on my good fortune and how I had been so blessed to have Mum and Dad to care for me over the years.

The funeral took place as planned at noon on Friday. My brother-in-law came over to Fairford to attend, and drove me back to Wokingham before my departure to Auckland. The funeral service helped me to give a sense of closure; for Dad, as well as Mum. They had chosen a grave together in the small local churchyard of St Thomas of Canterbury. The small neo-Gothic church was packed with mourners. As the service ended the coffin was carried out towards the open graveside. The mourners gathered outside and sheltered in the churchyard under a cluster of dark green yew trees. Carefully, the light oak casket was lowered into the damp earth. Afterwards I stood alone beside the open grave, looking down on Mum's lonely coffin. It lay in peace on a soft bed of gold, yellow and brown autumn leaves. They were both at last in peace, together.

Epilogue

I started writing this memoir at the beginning of 2014. Reflecting back to the key events that shaped my life, finding my birth mother Enda in 1991 was a momentous event. Our reunion produced great joy, but it eventuated in a period when I was also experiencing personal tragedy. My adopted sister Monica passed away the same year and a year later Mum and Dad died, within a few months of each other.

After Mum's funeral I returned to Auckland. As I grieved and reflected on my loss, I continued an exchange of letters with my birth mother which we had established back in October 1991. Mother and I had only spent a few days together and these letters were the early building blocks of getting to know each other. From the beginning we always started our letters to each other with a term of endearment; *My Dear Mother,* or *My Dear Son.* Both of us kept the letters we received from each other, perhaps prompted by the fear of losing each other again, and that's how it felt to me.

In mid-1993, Mother came out to stay with us in New Zealand for a holiday. Mother's first visit provided the opportunity for her and my family in New Zealand to get to know each other. Over the years Mother came out to stay with us many times. My two children saw her more as a distant aunt, not as their grandmother. I saw them develop a close affection for her over the years. Nicola and Matthew were certain of their ethnicity and welcomed Enda into our family as my mother, but not as my mum. Judy and I saw this as a completely natural reaction, reinforced by my wish to separate the reality of my adoptive mum from my birth mother. I saw both my Mother and my Mum as first among equals.

***

A few years later, after meeting her in England and her subsequent visit to us in Auckland in 1993, I was lucky to find a new job based in Australia. The position was located in Brisbane and was for tenure of two years. Judy travelled over from Auckland every few months and I returned home to Auckland for a week every couple of months. My fortnightly correspondence with Mother continued unabated. In one exchange of letters I suggested that a holiday in Brisbane would be a wonderful chance for her and me to spend time together alone.

Mother jumped at the opportunity. Looking back to 1996, the time we spent alone together in Australia was very special. It gave us the opportunity to relate as mother and son. We grew to know each other much better after five years and my memories of that special time together in Brisbane were filled with laughter and a great sense of fun.

***

In September 2000 Judy and I travelled to England on holiday. We spent a week in Ireland with my brother-in-law and sister-in-law based in Kinsale, County Cork. The popular coastal town was our first exposure together of Irish hospitality and culture. Before we left New Zealand, I had mentioned to Mother we were planning a holiday in Ireland. She suggested I spend a few days with her in Waterford, her original home town.

The opportunity was too good to miss. After spending a week in Kinsale we drove to Waterford where I left Albert, Judy and her sister, who travelled back to England by ferry.

My mother and her three sisters had grown up in a small terrace house in Ferrybank, an outer suburb of Waterford. The house was close to the banks of the meandering River Suir. The semi-detached house was located down a long narrow lane. Surrounded by lush green farmland, the property looks out towards the wide river. The gardens were full of rambling plants, shaded by mature trees. Piles of sawn logs, as well as cut tree branches were stacked against a stone wall fronting the home. Built of brick, the walls were screened with cement pebbledash, while the roof was covered in grey slate tiles. An abandoned single railway line separated the river from the property.

My grandfather had rented the house, while working on the railroad. When he retired, he and his wife purchased the dwelling from his employer and they both lived there until they died. The house was left to my mother's only brother, whose home was in Los Angeles. He spent most summers in Ferrybank and when the house was vacant, he provided the use of the house to his siblings.

Although my mother had spent her childhood in Ireland, she lived all of her adult life in England. However, her Irish heritage was an essential part of her identity. From her Irish brogue, through to her Catholic faith, she was infatuated with Irish culture. Like many of her compatriots, Mother was a great story teller. She constructed a narrative full of myths and memories to convey traditions that were important to her.

Staying with her in her family home, gave me a strong feeling of connection with previous generations. One morning I recall Mother waving the Irish flag in jest outside the front door. I had been out for a walk and seeing her in her blue dressing gown waving the flag, seemed like a gesture of invitation to muster. She had a wicked sense of humour.

On the Sunday before we left Kinsale, Mother and I went to Mass at the local church. Her father and mother were buried in the graveyard and seeing the inscriptions on my grandparents' headstone provided another connection to my ethnicity. Seeing photographs of family in the house with physical characteristics I recognised in myself, was significant in understanding where I had come from. While I was staying there I slept every night in my grandfather's room. Each night before going to bed, Mother and I would natter for hours about all things under the sun; I began to feel completely at home. It was about time, it was my fifty-fifth year.

***

Many people say, as you grow older time travels more quickly. It certainly feels that way. Over the next thirteen years Mother and I spent many times together, both in England and New Zealand. She would come and stay with us and I would take time out when on holiday in England with Judy to stay with her. Living in different countries so far apart ironically intensified our relationship. The time Mother and I spent together was quality time; we savoured every moment we had.

During late-2010, Mother was diagnosed with a form of dementia. She was living alone in sheltered accommodation and had for many years looked after herself. Eventually, after the prognosis was confirmed, she moved to fulltime residential care. The letters between us stopped. She was unable to write and as the months went on, even access by telephone was beyond her. The last telephone call I made to her was a couple of years later.

When she asked who was calling, I replied. 'It's your son, Paul, from New Zealand.'

Mother replied in a confused tone. 'I don't have a son in New Zealand. Who's calling?'

I repeated my statement and the response was the same. I put down the phone. It was my last phone call to her. I didn't want to cause her any more anxiety. It was so sad.

Dementia is such a distressing condition. To watch the disintegration of a person's personality whom you love is like the elements of a beautiful picture fading before your eyes. The pixels begin to fade and in the end, you're left with just a memory.

The last time I saw Mother was in late September 2013. I was staying with my younger brother Vince, and his wife Margaret, in Oxfordshire. Their home was close to Mother's rest home. While I was staying with them, Vince and I went to visit her. We drove the short distance to Aylesbury where Mother resided. After spending some time negotiating the facility's security system, we entered the entrance lobby and took the elevator to the second floor. Outside the lift were open doors, leading into a large residents' lounge. Mother was seated in a high back chair and looked frail. Vince and I walked towards her, and when she noticed us, she returned a welcoming smile.

'Hello Mum,' said Vince. 'Look who's come to see you.'

He leaned down to kiss her and we both sat down beside her.

'Hello Mother. How are you?' I said, looking up to her face.

Mother returned my gaze, smiling contentedly. Her familiar thin white hair straggled across the side of her face. She was totally at ease and relaxed, yet she had no idea who I was.

'Hello,' she replied affectionately.

I had expected she would be unable to recognise me. It had been three years since we had that last telephone call. Although it was a surprise seeing her in the flesh with no sense of recognition, because she looked so happy and content, it helped to ease the pain.

We stayed talking for some time. Mother could converse, but the depth of the conversation had no regard for the characters in it. Just before we left, Vince said, 'Mum we're going now. We're going to the pub for a drink.'

With a chuckle and a glint in her eye she replied, 'Why are you two going for a drink then?'

Smiling back, Vince said, 'Because we just thought we'd have one Mum!'

'Go on then, you'd better be going,' she said, in her soft Irish brogue.

We both gave her a big hug and waved as she sat back in her chair. When we reached the lift, I looked back. What I saw was a frail old lady, who had no idea anybody had just been to see her. Yet, she looked perfectly contented and happy in a world of her own.

The next day we called again. The situation was the same; she had no idea who we really were. We enjoyed a cup of tea together and some of Mother's favourite sweet biscuits. I would never see her again.

Over the next few months her health declined further. Towards the end of January 2014 I received a phone call from my brother, Vince. It was the call we all dread. As soon as I picked up the phone and heard the tone in Vince's voice I knew; Mother had passed away.

As I reflect back to that moment, I am so thankful for the time I had spent with her. If I had to describe her in a few words it would be that she was an affectionate lady, who was upfront and straight as a die, with a wicked sense of humour – what you saw, was what you got.

Mother had given me life. I'd lost her, and had found her again. And in the end, I had lost her once more when she was unable to recognise me. Yet, her memory will remain with me forever. The journey we embraced together consolidated my identity; I now know who I am. For Mother, re-establishing our connection after so many years apart, gave her peace and joy and a whole new lease on life. I am for ever thankful for finding Enda.